SURVIVAL IN THE AUSTRALIAN OUTDOORS

Doug Ainslie

Produced for Gary Allen Pty Ltd
by Allan Cornwell

Designed by S.W.A.M.P.
Illustrated by Jeremy T. Newman
Typeset by Half A Sec Business Support Services, Frankston
Printed by Griffin Paperbacks

Cover design by Allan Cornwell

ISBN 1-875702-26-1

First published in Australia by
Gary Allen Pty Ltd
9 Cooper Street
Smithfield
New South Wales 2164

CONTENTS

Introduction v
1 Water 1
2 Shelter 11
3 Fire 17
4 First aid 25
5 Food 49
6 Weather maps and signs 61
7 Natural disasters 69
8 Temperature extremes 79
9 Dangerous creatures 87
10 Direction finding 105
11 Vehicles 117
12 Signals 125

INTRODUCTION

Your survival may depend on many factors – preparedness, knowledge and skill, strength and fitness, and your state of mind. Strangely enough, it is your state of mind that is likely to have the biggest influence on whether you live or not. Without the will to live, your equipment, knowledge, skill, strength and fitness are almost worthless. A person with a positive attitude will be calm, confident, determined, optimistic and sensible. With these attributes that person is less likely to panic, despair, make hasty or foolish decisions or give up. Faced with fear, pain, exhaustion, thirst, hunger, extreme temperatures, loneliness or boredom they will be determined to live and will do everything possible to survive their ordeal. Everyone has heard extraordinary stories of endurance and survival; in each one, mental attitude is vital.

Other survival prerequisites that you can carry with you at all times include knowledge, skills and fitness. We have already considered mental fitness. If you are physically fit you will be better able to survive the stresses that you face – injury; lack of water, food or shelter; great physical effort or endurance. As part of your physical fitness, you should have acquired a range of survival skills before you are ever likely to use them. Can you light a fire, build a shelter out of bush materials, put out a fire, heat water or cook food outdoors, fish or hunt, walk all day, prepare bush food?

Knowledge is another survival essential. Can you read the sun, moon or stars to establish directions; can you tell edible fungi and plants from inedible or poisonous varieties; do you know how to give first aid, what the human body needs to stay alive?

Preparedness includes any preparation that makes you disaster-proof, such as gaining knowledge, skills and fitness, as well as any preparation before a particular event or journey that is likely to increase your chances of survival. Do a first aid course and then keep your knowledge and skills up-to-date with refresher courses. Make sure you can identify edible foods before you have to rely on them. Learn to use a compass and map from an expert and not from a book. Finally, practise your skills and refresh your knowledge and understanding of survival technique.

Emergency kit

The following list can be altered to suit your particular needs. Some items are more important than others, so if you have very little space, think carefully about what you can include.

- ❑ Beta light
- ❑ Candle
- ❑ Compass
- ❑ Energy food (chocolate/sweets, dehydrated meat, hard tack, scroggin, etc.
- ❑ Fishing line, hooks and sinkers
- ❑ Flint (fire-lighter)
- ❑ Garbage bag
- ❑ Knife
- ❑ Magnifying glass (fire-lighter)
- ❑ Map
- ❑ Matches (waterproofed)
- ❑ Medical kit (see below)
- ❑ Mirror
- ❑ Needle and thread (large/strong)
- ❑ Nylon cord (10 m)
- ❑ Pencil and waterproof paper
- ❑ Plastic bags or condoms (for water)
- ❑ Saw, flexible
- ❑ Signals (copy of Morse and ground to air code)
- ❑ Snare wire
- ❑ Solar still (plastic sheet and tube)
- ❑ Torch
- ❑ Water purifying tablets
- ❑ Whistle
- ❑ Space blanket or other survival bag

Medical kit

The medications you take will depend on the trip you plan, the country you will be entering, and the hazards you are likely to face, and any special needs you or someone in your party may have. This list is basic, and can be supplemented to meet particular needs. Pack all drugs carefully in air- and watertight containers labelled with dosage information and expiry dates in waterproof ink.

- ❑ Antibiotics (full course)
- ❑ Antihistamine (for allergies)
- ❑ Anti-irritant solution (for stings or bites)
- ❑ Antimalaria tablets (if appropriate)
- ❑ Antiseptic solution
- ❑ Bandages (e.g., conforming, triangular, roller, elastic)
- ❑ Diarrhoea treatment (incl. electrolite powder, etc.)
- ❑ Dressings (e.g., sterile combine, sterile non-adherent, large and small wound dressings)
- ❑ First aid manual
- ❑ Needles
- ❑ Pain killers (for mild to moderate pain)
- ❑ Potassium permanganate (add to water – pink will sterilise, dark pink is antiseptic, red treats fungal diseases)
- ❑ Safety pins
- ❑ Salt tablets
- ❑ Scalpel blades
- ❑ Space blanket (i.e. foil rescue blanket)
- ❑ Sticking plasters
- ❑ Tweezers
- ❑ Water sterilising tablets
- ❑ Sutures (butterfly)

SUMMARY

- ❑ Do not drink urine or sea water, ever.
- ❑ Do not drink polluted water or radiator water containing antifreeze or anti-rust treatments.
- ❑ Do not drink less water than your body loses each day.
- ❑ Conserve the water in your body:
  - sweat as little as possible
  - wear loose pale clothing, open slightly for ventilation
  - do anything active after dark
  - lie still in the shade above the ground
  - breathe through your nose
  - don't smoke or drink alcohol
  - don't talk
  - eat as little food as possible
  - make the most of breezes
  - at sea keep clothes wet.
- ❑ Mop up dew with cloths.
- ❑ Collect rain with sheets or in holes.
- ❑ Filter and purify surface water by boiling, etc.
- ❑ Underground water can be found at low points. Dig it up after dark:
  - at the bottom of cliffs, valleys, creek beds, soaks, dams, etc.
  - where there is green vegetation
  - behind the first sand dune or in dune hollows
  - above the high tide mark
  - above clay barriers.
- ❑ Extract water from vines, roots, saplings, succulents, palms.
- ❑ Rig up solar stills.
- ❑ Collect condensation from plants in plastic bags.
- ❑ Melt deep snow a little at a time; or ice.
- ❑ Fresh white sea ice is salt; melt clean aged blue ice.
- ❑ Be alert to signs of water:
  - converging tracks of humans or herbivores
  - low swift-flying seed-eating birds at dawn and dusk
  - ant trails
  - bees, flies, etc.
- ❑ Don't risk diarrhoea or vomiting.

1 WATER

Water is scarce throughout most of the continent of Australia, and temperatures are high for at least some months each year. These conditions can easily combine to threaten your survival. In temperatures of 38°C with no physical activity during the day, a person will survive for only three to five days without water. After 6-8 litres of fluid are lost, death is almost unavoidable.

Water and the human body

The human body is roughly 70 per cent water – without water, people can survive for only a few days. It is an essential part of every cell of the body; the liquid part of blood and lymph; essential to digestion; dissolves wastes; distributes and regulates heat in the body and helps cool the body through perspiration. The water concentration in the human body remains more or less constant, even though under normal circumstances we are taking in water and losing it in various ways most of the time. Each day the body loses water as water vapour from the lungs, in urine and faeces, and through the skin. Water can also be lost through vomiting, serious blisters and diarrhoea. On a hot day, the body can lose a great deal of water in sweat alone. This water must be replaced or the person will die.

The human body is able to regulate water loss in some ways but not in others. For example, on a hot day when a person has drunk little, less urine will be passed. But even a person dying of dehydration will still lose water through sweating. It is helpful to remember this if you find yourself short of water. *The water you lose from your body* will affect your survival, not just the amount of water available for you to drink.

Minimise water loss

To minimise loss of water through sweating, stay as cool as you can and do as little as you can. Lie in the shade during the day, and if you must move, move slowly. Do not take off your clothes – they will protect you from sunburn (the resultant blisters and sweat would increase water loss) and slow the rate at which your sweat evaporates. Open your clothes a little to allow for ventilation so you don't become overheated. If you have a choice, wear light-coloured clothes. Make the most of any breezes. Try to avoid vomiting or diarrhoea. Don't smoke or drink alcohol. Eat as little as possible, especially fat and protein (water is needed to digest food). Talk as little as possible and breathe through your nose not your mouth. Don't lie on hot earth or other surfaces; if you can raise yourself above the ground you will probably be able to keep cooler. At sea, keep your clothes wet. Any activities should be undertaken at night when it is cooler.

If water is scarce, drink your share in small sips, no matter how much you want to gulp it down. If you drink too rapidly you may vomit and lose precious fluid.

Never drink sea water or urine. Either can be distilled to provide fresh water, but without this treatment they are deadly.

Ground water

Water in rivers, creeks, dams, lakes, puddles or crevices may or may not be fit for drinking, but if you have no choice, try to reduce the chances of becoming ill by filtering and/or purifying the water.

Stagnant water is more likely to be polluted than running water. In central Australia lakes are often salt, and the water must be distilled to obtain clean drinking water. If a pool contains animal bones or there

Filter water first.

are bones nearby, or if the pool is not surrounded by green vegetation, it is probably polluted. If there are mineral deposits at the edge of the water it may be alkaline and therefore dangerous.

At the very least, filter water through a handkerchief or leave it to stand so that solids can settle out (this may take many hours). In desperate circumstances, if you do not have a container, you can place a handkerchief on the surface of the water before you drink. Water can also be filtered through sand or soil if you have enough water and the sand or soil has not been polluted by animals. Allow the water to seep through half a metre of sand or soil and into a hole.

Boil water for 5 minutes or use water purification tablets. Eight drops of 2½ per cent solution of iodine will purify 1 litre of water if it is left to stand for 10 minutes. Similarly, 1 or 2 small Condy's crystals allowed to stand for 30 minutes in a litre of water will purify it against many of the less dangerous organisms, but boiling is always safer.

Rain and dew

When rain is in the offing, set out anything you can to collect as much of it as possible. If you are without any useful supplies, dig a hole and line it with clay. Sheets of bark and even large leaves can be used to

catch water and funnel it into containers. Any sheet metal or canvas or plastic will collect water. If you can't rig up a sling or other 'container', then dig a hole and line it with your sheeting.

Don't forget dew – it may be all that keeps you alive. Anything metal can be used to collect dew. Use a clean cloth to mop up as much as possible and suck it, or wring it into a container. Dew can also be mopped off vegetation (people have even tied cloths round their ankles and walked through dewy grass and undergrowth) or any smooth surface, and collected in a plastic-lined hole. If you have something smooth or shiny, place it in the hole; dew will collect on it and run off onto the plastic.

Finding water

If there is no water in sight, remember the way water behaves as you set out to search for it. Water runs downhill, so look for it at the lowest point in the landscape – at the bottom of hills or cliffs, in valleys or gullies. Creeks and streams can run underground for part of their length, and water can lie beneath the surface in a creek bed long after all surface water has disappeared. Try digging in such places, but only

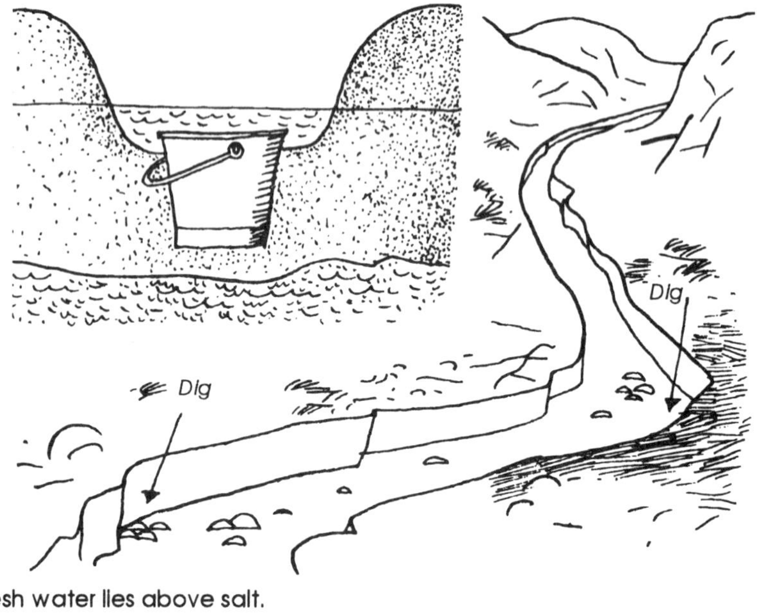

Fresh water lies above salt.

where there are signs of moisture such as green vegetation. Do not waste energy and body fluids digging unless these are present. When you do dig, stop when you see that the soil or sand is damp and allow the water to seep into the hole you have made. In watercourses, dig on the outside of bends and at the lowest point. Remember also that clay can form an impermeable layer beneath sand, trapping water in the sand above it which can be drained into a container.

Springs are often marked by unusually green grass or other vegetation, so be alert for these signs. They may also indicate a place where water lay until recently, so try digging there.

By the sea, fresh water can sometimes be found above the high tide mark, behind the first sand dune or in hollows in the dunes. Make sure you don't dig too deep or you may come upon salt water and ruin your supply of fresh water. Generally fresh water will lie above salt water if the two have combined.

Living indicators

Animals, insects and people can guide you to water if you know what to look for. If you are in country where people are likely to know about the presence of water, follow their tracks too. If the water source has been covered over to conserve it, replace the cover after you have drunk.

Herbivores need to drink regularly, so follow converging tracks downhill. Seed-eating birds also need to drink regularly, and will head for water in the morning or evening, flying straight and low. Meat-eating animals or birds and reptiles are not good indicators because they get moisture from their prey.

Insects such as bees, ants and flies are usually not far from water, and a beehive is rarely more than 5 or 6 kilometres from a source of water. Flies may be even closer to water, and columns of ants that are not heading for prey may be on the way to water, especially if they are climbing a tree. Look carefully for water pooled in a fork or hollow.

Animals as water sources

Animal bodies contain water, and many flesh-eating animals derive most of their fluid from the bodies of their prey. If you are able to fish, look for water along the spine of fish, especially large ones. To do this, gut the fish then, holding it carefully on its back, remove the backbone to expose the liquid. But beware – other body fluid in the fish is protein-rich and will draw fluid from *your* body as you digest it.

Certain desert frogs store water in their bodies, but they must first be dug up then the water squeezed out of them.

Animal eyes also contain water that can be sucked out.

Plants and water

Plants not only may signal the presence of water, they may also be a source or container of drinkable water. As a general rule, drink sap only if it is clear and tasteless – milky sap may be toxic. If you suspect that the plant itself may cause skin irritation, allow the water to drip from it into your mouth or a container.

Water-containing plants

Look for plants with hollows or crevices where water may collect, and check the base of leaves for droplets. Sometimes water is stored in the tissue of plants and trees, the most famous examples being the baobab and the bottle tree. The spongy tissue beneath the bark of the baobab can be chewed to extract moisture, and a V-shaped cut into the sapwood of the bottle tree should provide water. Hold a leaf at the base of the cut to direct water into your mouth or a container. Remember how water behaves and look for plants in valleys – they will contain more water than those on higher ground. There will also be more water in the early morning than after a long hot day. Drink fluid from plants within a day – it may go bad if it is stored.

The roots of certain trees such as bloodwood, she-oak or casuarina, and some eucalypts can yield water. This is more likely in arid regions whereas in wetter more temperate regions saplings rather than roots will hold water. Drain water in the early morning because trees are more likely to have stored up water overnight.

If the roots are close to the surface, tear up a length, cut it into shorter pieces (1 metre will do) and prop the lengths in a bark or other container so the water can be collected. Alternatively, remove the bark and shave the wood so that water can be squeezed out.

Choose a sapling with a good healthy crown and a diameter of 10 to 15 cm. Try melaleucas (tea-tree), stringy barks or paper barks as well as eucalypts. A 5 metre sapling should supply about half a litre of water. Cut it off at ground level, then just below the branches with a diagonal cut. Turn the sapling upside down and prop it against a tree or rock so that the liquid can drain out into a container or rock hollow. When the liquid no longer flows, cut the sapling in half and drain both halves.

Vines can supply water. Cut them into 1 metre lengths and prop them in a container to drain. If the water ceases, cut a section off the top of the vine and it should start again. Alternatively, cut a notch high on the vine *then* cut off the bottom of that vine near the ground to allow the water to drip out. When the water stops dripping, repeat the process with another vine. If you reverse the order of the cuts, water will run up the vine.

Certain palms such as the buri, nipa, sugar and, of course, the coconut can yield fluid, although milk from ripe coconuts is a laxative and may cause you to lose more fluid than you take in. Locate a flowering stalk, bend it down and cut off the tip. Renew the cut twice a day to keep the liquid flowing.

Cacti and other succulents contain water. Crush the fleshy leaves in a container.

Ice and snow

If you intend to melt ice or snow for drinking water, choose ice – it will provide you with more water for less heat. If you must use snow, dig below the surface and put only a little in the container to heat, gradually adding more.

At sea, use only aged ice – fresh sea ice, which is white and rough, is salt. Aged ice is blue with weathered edges, but beware of any ice that may have been splashed with salt water or spray.

Condensation and distillation

Plastic bags and sheets usually cause more trouble environmentally than they are worth, but when water is scarce they can be extremely useful.

Water from foliage

Tie a plastic bag around a fresh leafy branch and secure it tightly at the top, allowing a corner of the bag to hang below the leaves to collect water. Moisture will evaporate from the leaves and condense within the bag, trickling down the sides. With bushes, dig a shallow trench around the plant and line it with plastic, weighed down with stones if necessary. Bring the plastic up and over the bush, suspending it clear of the foliage. If any leaves touch the plastic, water will run down them onto the ground rather than down the plastic 'tent' and into the trench.

Water can also be drawn from cut foliage using either of these methods. If you put it in a large plastic bag, line the bottom with clean stones first so the water can collect amongst them. Keep the leaves away from the sides of the bag, and try to make a tent by supporting the top on a padded stick or tying it up with a piece of string. Alternatively, foliage can be used as a source of moisture in a bush or solar still.

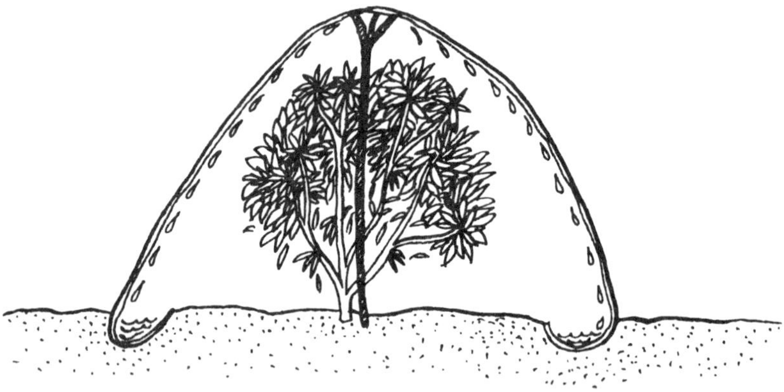

Bush or solar still

Distillation purifies liquid that would otherwise be undrinkable because of salts or pollution. Heat causes water vapour to evaporate from the liquid; it then condenses into its liquid form which can be collected and drunk. A simple still can be built and used to process urine, salt water, polluted water, or to draw clean water out of foliage, grasses or other vegetable matter.

Basically, you need an inverted cone of plastic sheeting (1-2 square metres is good) above a container to collect the clean water. If you have a large container, you can spread the plastic over that and place a stone in the centre to create the inverted cone, or you can dig a hole and anchor the plastic round the edges with large stones and earth. Within the still you can simply have damp earth, or vegetation, or a container of water that is unsuitable for drinking. The container that will collect the clean water should be positioned exactly under the lowest point of the plastic. If you have the foresight to include a length of plastic tubing in your gear, this can be positioned to draw off the water without disturbing the still. Otherwise, open the still at night when you are less likely to lose water vapour. You should also dig your still at night to reduce fluid loss through sweat. Be prepared to make a number of these stills to provide enough water, and replenish them when the water vapour begins to diminish.

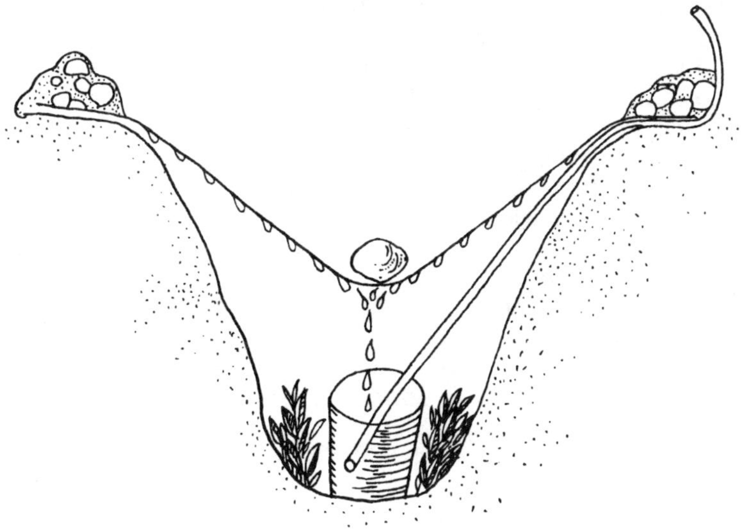

SUMMARY

- ❑ Choose a sheltered campsite near fuel.
- ❑ Position the entrance to your shelter cross-wind.
- ❑ Look for natural shelter.
- ❑ Make use of your vehicle but avoid it in the heat.
- ❑ Do not cook inside a vehicle.
- ❑ Allow adequate ventilation in any shelter.
- ❑ Small shelters are easier to warm.
- ❑ Avoid sites that are hazardous due to:
  - exposure to wind
  - damp or cold
  - risk of flooding
  - insects or animals
  - falling timber
  - lightning
  - water noise masking danger or rescuers
- ❑ Don't sleep on the ground.
- ❑ Don't sleep for long periods in the snow.

2 SHELTER

If conditions are extreme enough, lack of shelter can mean death within as little as three hours. In less severe conditions it can still mean the difference between whether you survive or not. Some form of shelter can be found, or constructed from materials at hand, in most situations, and so long as you remember a few simple rules your chances of survival will be enhanced.

Types of shelter

The type of shelter you have will depend on the circumstances in which you find yourself, the climate and your needs. If you had planned to go into the bush, then you have the opportunity to take a good-quality tent with you. If you suddenly find yourself stranded, you may have to rely on material at hand. If you suspect you will be stuck in the one spot for some time, it will be worth building a sturdy, comfortable shelter. If the climate is likely to endanger your survival, you will have to build a suitable shelter to protect yourself.

Modern tents are light, sturdy, well-designed, and capable of protecting you from most bad weather. Before you buy or hire, ask the advice of someone in a reputable shop. Tell them where and how you intend to use the tent. Will you ever need to camp in snow? How many people must it accommodate? Are you likely to camp in it for long periods? How will the tent cope with prolonged bad weather? With wind? How much headroom is there? How much room per person? How heavy is it to carry? How quickly can it be pitched and taken down? Is it insect and animal proof? How much ventilation is there for hot weather? How easy is it to see if you are lost in the bush? In the desert? In the snow?

Camp sites

Choosing a good safe camp site can be vital. Whenever possible, allow yourself plenty of daylight in which to choose a site and to clear and level it. In the dark you could stumble into a bull ants nest or worse. You should be near enough to any water to make collecting it relatively easy, but not so close that the water endangers your camp. Do not site your shelter at the lowest point of a clearing, in a dry watercourse, right beside a river or body of water; if it rains, or the creek or river rises, your camp could be washed out. The sound of water covers other sounds that could indicate danger or rescue. Similarly, water often attracts insects, snakes and troublesome animals. Check also that you have not camped across tracks that indicate a favourite route to water.

Wind can ruin a camp site and increase the chill factor, so site your camp where there is shelter, not on the top or the side of a hill exposed to prevailing winds. When you set up a tent, the wind should blow across the mouth of the tent or at worst from behind the tent, never directly into it.

Cold damp air collects in valleys and hollows, so avoid them whenever possible, unless cold is not a problem.

In the Australian bush, limbs can fall from trees on a still day, so if possible, do not set up camp beneath trees. If this is not possible, check for dead trees or dead branches in surrounding trees. Tall solitary trees are, perhaps, more likely to be struck by lightning, so they too should be avoided. However, camping near trees does provide shelter and fuel.

The base of cliffs or steep eroded hillsides may not be suitable because of the risk of landslides or falling rocks.

Lastly, check that you are not camping near an insect nest. Bees, ants or wasps can all be dangerous when disturbed. If you are in an area where there are dangerous animals, think about their habitat and try to avoid places they may pass by or where they may be.

Emergency shelter

If you are suddenly stranded away from shelter, you will have to make do with whatever is at hand. If you have a vehicle, that can probably provide you with better and safer shelter than anything else. You will also be easier to find if you stay near your vehicle. Avoid sleeping in your vehicle in hot weather – you will lose valuable moisture and could suffer heat exhaustion. Do not cook inside either or you could poison yourself with fumes.

If you are stranded without a vehicle, look first for natural shelters such as overhanging rock ledges, caves, a large hollow tree or log, etc. Make sure that there are no dangerous inhabitants there already. If you find a cave, do not go too deeply into it in case you become lost, and check that you will not be trapped by a rock fall. The same applies if you are sheltering under an overhang or cliff.

If you have to rig up a makeshift shelter, try to dig a trench around it to collect and divert any run-off if it rains. A simple shelter and

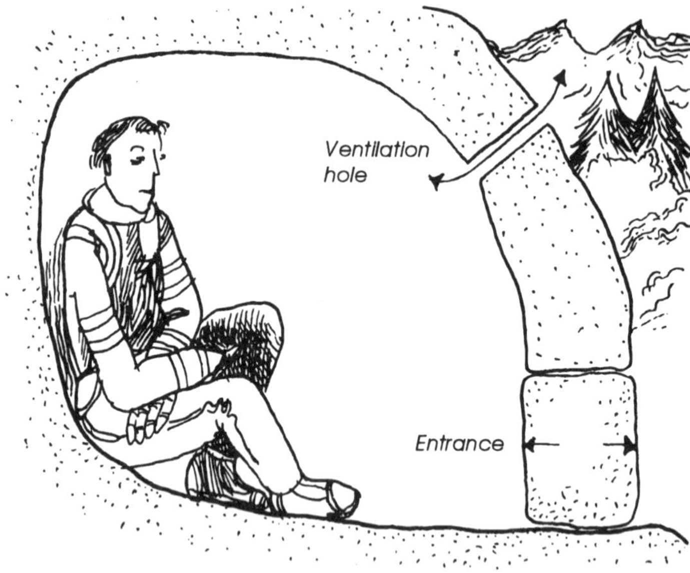

Snow cave.

windbreak can be constructed from fallen timber and branches propped against a fallen log or large rocks. If your 'roof' is steeply pitched, more rain will run off it. Collect dry bracken or grasses to insulate you from the cold earth and spread them inside your shelter. Similarly, make your shelter small so that it is easier to keep warm. Wind and wet are your enemies in a cold climate.

If you are stranded in the snow try to get below the treeline where there will be fuel for a fire. You may also find shelter beneath a fallen branch or tree, but make sure that it is not likely to fall any further. Collect branches or anything that will keep you up off the snow. Protect yourself as much as possible from wind and moisture.

If you risk exhausting yourself or someone in your party, give up the attempt to reach the treeline and find shelter in the snow. Keeping out of the wind is most important, as is keeping dry. If the snow is dry and compact, you can hollow out a snow cave. Position the entrance at the bottom of the cave so that any heat is trapped inside your shelter. Smooth the surface inside so that it is less likely to drip on you. Try to keep dry; if you can line your cave with bushes or grasses to keep yourself up off the snow, so much the better. Huddle together if there are a number of you, and eat what food you have. Make sure your snow cave has some ventilation.

If you are stranded where heat is a problem, provide yourself with as much shade and ventilation as possible, and try to rig up a sleeping platform clear of the ground.

So much depends on what materials you have on hand, on the type of vegetation, on terrain and climate that it is difficult to be prescriptive. The following illustrations provide some ideas.

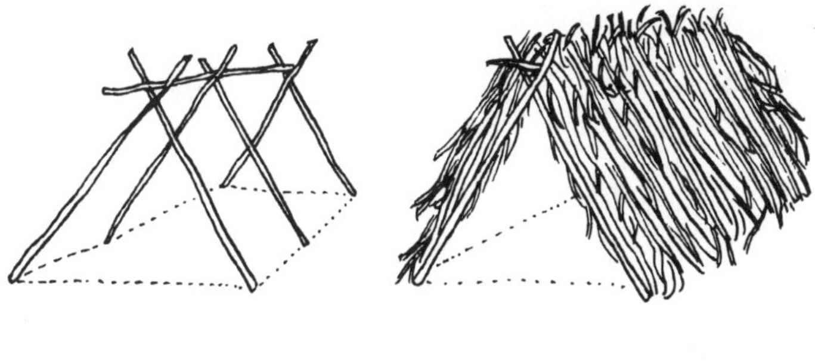

SUMMARY

- ❑ Carry firelighting equipment:
  - matches in a waterproof container
  - waterproof matches
  - cigarette lighter
  - flint and steel
  - magnifying glass, etc.
  - candle ends
  - tinder or firelighters
- ❑ Clear 1 metre around your fire site.
- ❑ Gather plenty of fuel first.
- ❑ Keep extra fuel dry under shelter.
- ❑ Build your fire carefully in a tepee form.
- ❑ Do not smother the fire with too much fuel.
- ❑ Do not waste fuel.
- ❑ Do not light a fire against a stump or tree.
- ❑ Use large rocks to reflect heat from the fire.
- ❑ Do not use wet or soft rocks around your fire.
- ❑ Keep yourself and your gear a safe distance from fire.
- ❑ Make sure your fire is completely out before you leave.

3 FIRE

Fire can help you survive by keeping you warm, purifying your water, keeping you and your possessions dry, cooking your food, signalling for help, cheering you up, keeping wild animals away, and driving out game or even bees.

Fire needs air, fuel and heat. Without any one of these the fire will go out. Keeping this in mind and building a fire well in the first place will save you a lot of trouble, energy and matches. In Australia, fire can also be a deadly enemy, so make sure your fire is positioned so that surrounding bush cannot catch fire. When you leave a camp-site to which you will not be returning, make sure the fire is thoroughly extinguished with water (watch out for rising steam which can give you a serious burn) or sand or soil heaped over it.

If you plan to bed down near a fire, make sure your gear is stowed safely away from the fire and that you are in no danger of being burned in your sleep by either rolling onto coals, by sparks igniting bedding if the wind rises, or by the fire spreading.

Siting a fire

Find a sheltered spot and clear the earth for 1 metre or so around your fire site so that the fire will not get away and start a bushfire. Do not site it under a tree or near anything flammable such as a dead stump or log. Building the fire near large rocks will provide shelter and radiant heat once the fire is going. If there are no large rocks you can build a reflector from logs opposite the fire to provide shelter and increase radiant heat, as well as encouraging the smoke to rise straight up.

In very wet or snowy conditions you can lay green logs covered with earth or stones on the surface and build your fire on that. A fire built on snow gradually sinks below the surface and smothers itself unless you dig air vents for it. In very windy conditions, build your fire in a trench or surround it with stones or rocks (these will retain heat and can keep your bed warm later). *Do not use wet rocks, slate, or soft or porous rocks around a fire; they can explode.*

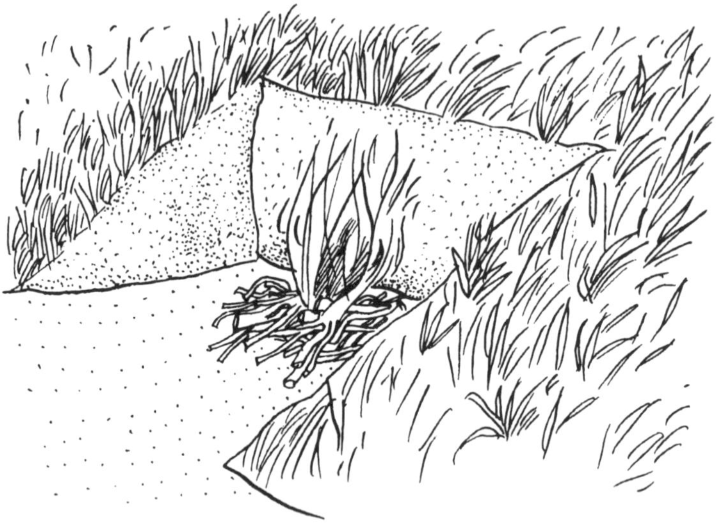

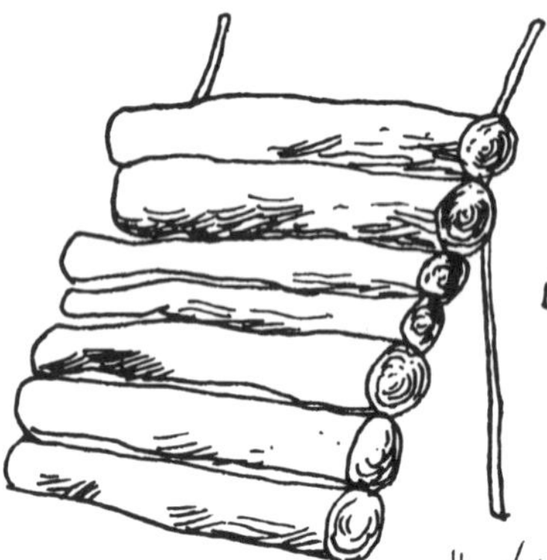

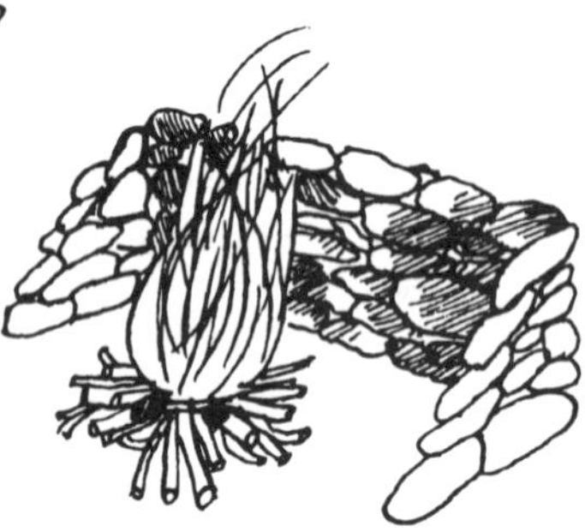

Fuel

If fuel is scarce, remember that you don't necessarily need a big fire. Food can be cooked on a fire no bigger than the bottom of your cooking pot.

Collect enough fuel to keep the fire going as long as necessary – it will be difficult or impossible to find more supplies after dark. If everything underfoot is wet, gather dead standing timber, loose bark and dead twigs from trees.

Conserve your energy by doing the least amount of work. Do not chop or saw logs if you can break them over a rock or in the fork of a tree. Large logs can be fed onto a fire bit by bit or suspended over the fire so that they burn through the middle.

You will need tinder, kindling, and larger branches and logs. If you suspect that you will be in the one place for some time, collect extra fuel and rig up a shelter to keep off the rain. Stack it so that air circulates to keep the fuel dry.

Tinder

Tinder is the fire's appetiser – it should tempt it. Anything that will catch alight from a spark, or very quickly, will do: very dry grass, bark, feathers or down, paper, wood shavings, wood dust from boring insects, pine needles, cotton fibres or fluff, etc.

Kindling

This is the entree for your fire and should consist of dry leaves, twigs and sticks. If it is impossible to find dry wood, you can cut through the wet outer layer of twigs to the dry wood inside, producing a 'feathered' fire stick that should catch quickly.

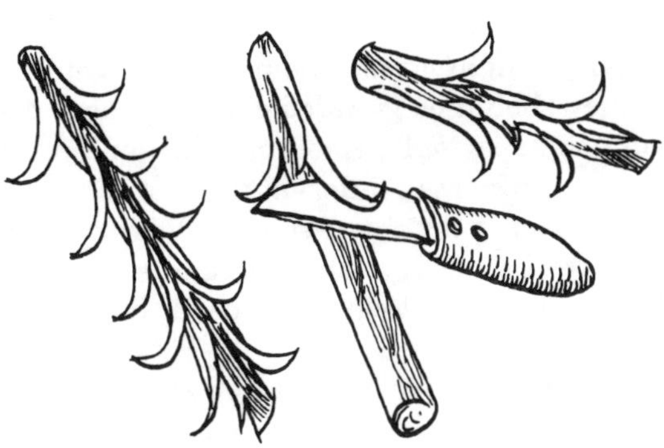

Larger fuel

This is the main meal for your fire and should consist of branches and logs ranging in size from not much thicker than your largest piece of kindling through to good hefty pieces of wood that will keep your fire alight for long periods. If most of your fuel is damp or wet, rig up a support of green timber near your fire or above it so you can dry fuel for later use. Lay larger logs beside the fire to dry out.

Setting a fire

Place tinder in the centre of your fire site and build a small tepee of the smallest and finest kindling you have. Add a few larger pieces of kindling and have your bigger pieces of wood nearby. The tepee shape will allow plenty of air into the fire and prevent it being smothered. Once the tinder has caught and the flames have reached the kindling, you can feed ever larger pieces of fuel onto the fire, until it is hot enough to take the biggest pieces without being smothered.

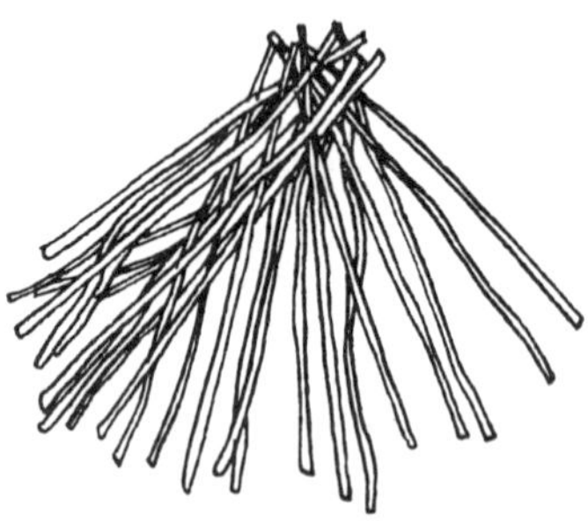

Starting a fire

Matches and lighters

Matches and cigarette lighters are the best way to start a fire, and if you have them they should be guarded carefully, kept dry in the case of matches, and used sparingly. Keep matches and striking sides in waterproof sealed containers in different parts of your clothing or gear so you are unlikely to lose your entire supply. Waterproof matches such as Greenlites are even better. If you have a candle, light it with a match and then use the candle to light whatever needs lighting – you will use far fewer matches.

If matches become damp for any reason, strike them with a short stabbing motion rather than a long scrape – they will light more readily.

If matches are in really short supply you can try splitting one and using the split portions instead of a whole match. Only do this to one match at a time until you are sure you can strike the split pieces. If you are taking a lighter, make sure you have plenty of fuel and spare flints.

Lenses

A lens from a magnifying glass, camera, telescope, binoculars or, in desperate circumstances, a curved piece of broken glass, can be used to focus the rays of the sun into a single spot which, when directed on tinder, will provide enough heat to ignite it. Hold the tiny bright spot of light steady in one place, shelter it from the wind and blow gently as it starts to catch.

Flints

Flints, or hard stones such as quartz or agate, can sometimes be picked up, or you can pack one in your gear. When they are struck against steel they make a spark which can ignite tinder. A little petrol dripped onto the tinder first will help it catch. Flints manufactured for gas and cigarette lighters are more effective.

Ammunition

Break open a round of ammunition and remove the shot. Pour half the powder onto the tinder. This can then be ignited with a flint. If you do not have a flint, stuff a small piece of rag into the cartridge and fire it into the ground or into the air. The smouldering cloth will be expelled and can be placed on the tinder.

Battery

You can get a spark out of a car or similar battery by winding the end of a piece of wire around one battery post and touching the other end to the other post. Remove the battery from the car before you attempt this. Alternatively you can attach a length of wire to each post and bring the ends close together above the tinder.

Friction

The idea of lighting a fire without matches may seem romantic until you try it, but it is difficult and takes a good deal of effort and skill. Nevertheless if there is no alternative, it can be done. Basically you have to rub two surfaces of wood together until enough heat is produced to light the tinder. Some techniques produce their own tinder; with others you add tinder. Some people believe that it is best to use hardwood and softwood together; however, you may not have the luxury of choice. Both pieces of wood should be very dry.

There are a number of different techniques involving a spindle that is rotated or scraped along a board. The latter technique involves cutting a groove in the baseboard then rubbing and scraping a piece of wood back and forth along it to produce tinder and eventually ignite it. The wood for the board should, ideally, produce tinder that is powdery or grainy; if it is stringy or fibrous it will be much harder to ignite.

Rotating a spindle to produce a spark works best if the board has been prepared. One technique is to cut a V-shaped hollow out of one end of the board and gouge a small depression at the point of the V. Tinder is placed between the arms of the V and the tip of the spindle in the depression. Another method involves gouging a depression at one end of the board and hollowing out the wood beneath it to accommodate the tinder. The spindle is then rotated in the depression until it pierces the wood and the friction allows a spark to drop through onto the tinder.

Rotating the spindle can be done by simply rolling it between your hands, working them down the spindle as you go to increase the pressure and friction. Alternatively, you can make a bow and wrap the string of the bow once around the spindle. Pressure can be applied to the top of the spindle by pressing down with a hollow stone or piece of wood (ideally lubricated with grease). The bow is then drawn back and forth, thus rotating the spindle. A little dry sand can be added to the depression to increase friction.

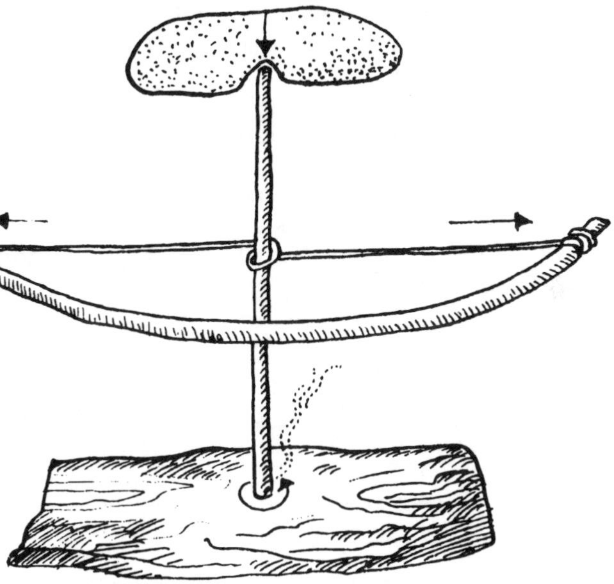

As the friction increases the tip of the spindle should start to glow red. Blow very gently to encourage the tinder to catch, and when it does so, continue to blow, adding a little more tinder until you are sure it will not go out.

Signal fires

Signalling is probably the only excuse for a big fire. If you want to attract attention during the day, smoke is usually more effective than fire. Establish a good hot fire, then lay some green branches over the flames, taking care not to smother the fire. You should get some good plumes of smoke. Allow the fire to recover before adding any more branches.

SUMMARY

- ❑ Ensure you and the injured person are safe from further injury.
- ❑ Check for consciousness.
- ❑ Establish and maintain breathing and heartbeat.
- ❑ Stop any bleeding.
- ❑ Cover any burns or wounds.
- ❑ Splint or immobilise broken bones.
- ❑ Treat for shock.
- ❑ Place an unconscious person in the coma position.
- ❑ Begin mouth-to-mouth resuscitation if breathing fails.
- ❑ If heartbeat fails, combine mouth-to-mouth and external cardiac compression.

First aider(s)	Patient	Compressions	Inflations	In seconds	Sequences per minute
1	Adult	15	2	15	4
1	Child	15	2	10	6
2	Adult	5	1	5	12
2	Child	5	1	3	20

4 FIRST AID

First aid can save lives, but if it is not delivered with care and skill it may result in further injury or even death. If possible, attend a good first aid course – you will learn more there than you possibly can from this or any other book. If you have no alternative and medical help is unreachable or will not arrive in time, stay calm and do what you can.

Make it safe

At the scene of an accident or disaster, it is easy to rush in without ensuring that you and the injured person(s) are safe from further danger or injury. Depending on the scene and the cause of injuries you should check that there is no risk from traffic, fire, gas, animals, debris, water, electrocution, further movement (in the case of spinal injury) and, now, AIDS, hepatitis and other infectious diseases.

If you can remove the danger from the injured person rather than having to move the person, then do so, taking care not to put yourself at risk.

If you must move them but you can examine them first without danger to yourself or the person, then do so. The main danger when moving an injured person is that a spinal injury could be exacerbated. If you suspect spinal injury, only move a person if they are in very serious danger. The way to move such a person is outlined below.

Conscious or unconscious

Shake the person firmly by the shoulders and ask them their name, then give them a simple command such as 'Squeeze my hand'. If they respond to a shouted or spoken command then they are conscious; if not, they are unconscious.

If the person is unconscious, check that they are breathing, that their airway is open, and that their heart is beating. If all these signs are satisfactory, turn the person into the coma position (see below).

If they are conscious, help them to sit or lie comfortably and watch them closely for at least a quarter of an hour, naturally attending to any injuries they may have sustained.

Breathing

If a person is not breathing, start resuscitation as soon as it is safe to do so. Mouth-to-mouth resuscitation is the best-known method, but mouth-to-nose works as well and is useful if the jaws are clenched or if you are working in deep water. With children and infants, your mouth covers their nose and mouth.

Mouth-to-mouth resuscitation

Place the person on their back on a solid surface, tilt back the head and open the mouth by holding the chin in the 'pistol grip' with your thumb and first finger only (this prevents you accidentally closing off the airway with your hand or fingers).

Take a deep breath and, sealing the person's nose either by pinching it (keep the head tilted back) or by pressing your cheek over it, place your mouth over the person's mouth and breathe air into the person's lungs. As you do so, watch their chest to see if it rises. *Do not* blow too hard or air will enter the stomach and may cause vomiting. If it does, and the stomach swells, *do not* try to force out the air.

Lift your mouth away a few centimetres and turn so that your ear is over their mouth and nose. Feel, look and listen for air escaping from the mouth and nose.

Repeat every two seconds or so for five breaths then check the carotid pulse (see below) to make sure the heart is still beating. If it is, continue resuscitation at the rate of one breath every four seconds until the person can breath unassisted. Keep checking the pulse every minute or two, and if it fails, begin external cardiac compression (cardiac massage) immediately.

Mouth-to-nose resuscitation

Proceed in the same way as you would for mouth-to-mouth resuscitation but push the person's bottom lip up against their top lip to seal their mouth. As the air escapes, pull back the lip but do not try to force open the mouth.

As you breathe into the nose, cover it from the bridge with your mouth, being careful not to press against the nostrils.

Resuscitating children and infants

Gently turn the child onto its back and remove any matter from the mouth and nose. Do not tilt back the head of babies because you could compress the airway rather than opening it. Cover the mouth and nose of children under one year old and puff air into them at the rate of one puff every three seconds. Use just enough force to raise the chest.

Check for a pulse after five puffs, then after a minute and then every two minutes. If there is no pulse, start external cardiac compression at once.

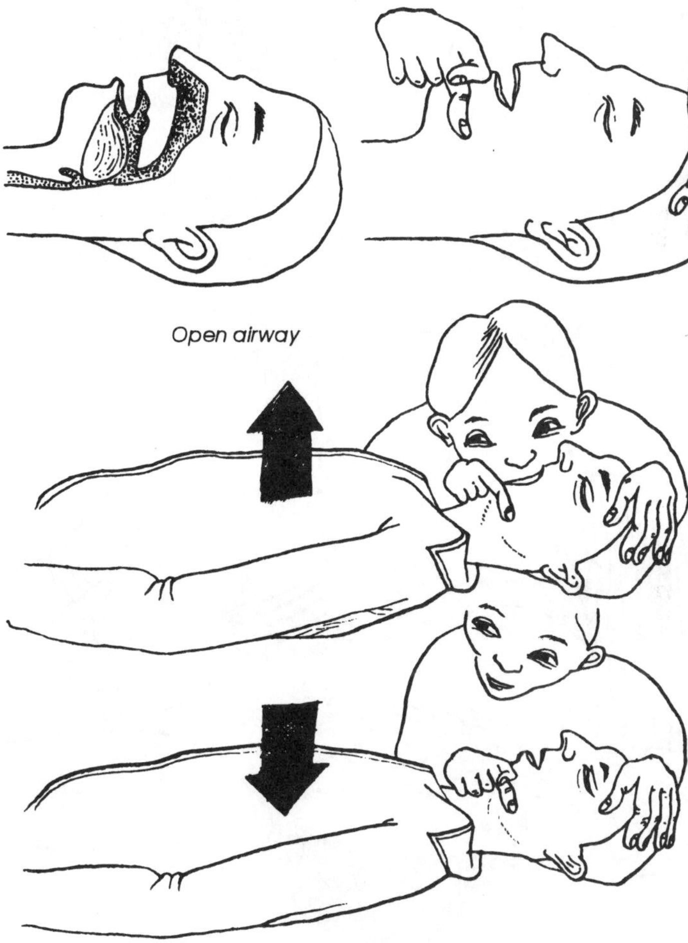

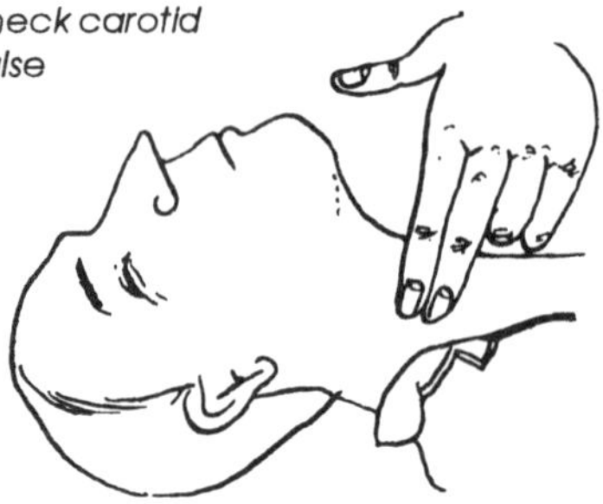

Check carotid pulse

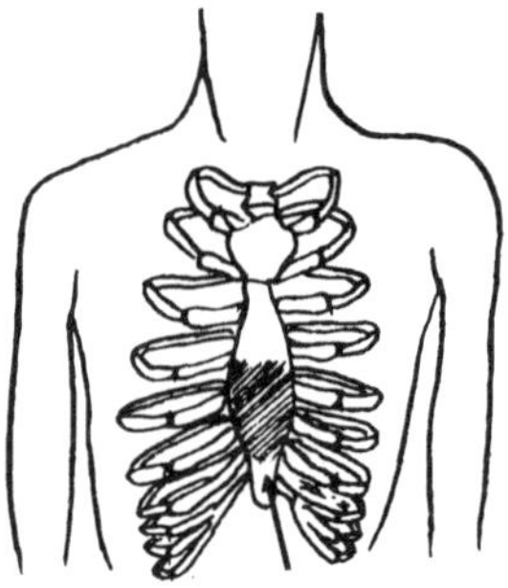

Position of hand

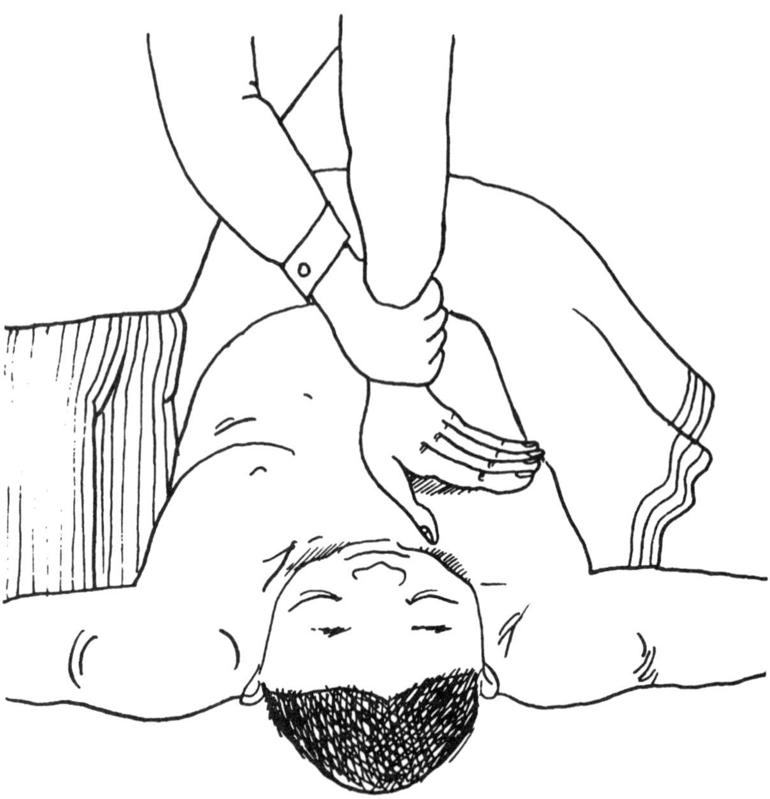

Heart beat

Check if there is a pulse in the carotid arteries. These lie on either side of the windpipe and can easily be felt under the jaw. If there is no pulse, begin external cardiac compression. It will circulate enough blood to keep the heart and brain alive until the body takes over itself or until help arrives. But you will also have to do mouth-to-mouth resuscitation so that the blood being pumped around the body during cardiac compression is oxygenated.

Heart and lungs

Working alone on an *adult* you will have to complete a sequence of fifteen compressions then two inflations in fifteen seconds; there will be four of these sequences per minute.

For *children* under eight you will have to work faster, with a sequence of fifteen compressions and two inflations every ten seconds; there will be six of these sequences per minute.

Working with another on an *adult* you should have a sequence of five compressions per inflation in five seconds; there will be twelve sequences per minute.

Working with another on a *child* you should have a sequence of five compressions per inflation in three seconds; there will be twenty sequences per minute.

Check the pulse after one minute then every two minutes after that. As soon as there is a pulse, stop cardiac compression; it should never be performed on a person with even a faint pulse because it could stop the heart.

External cardiac compression

To locate the correct place to apply pressure, first find the lower end of the breastbone (follow the lowest ribs to where they meet) then find the upper end between the collar-bones. Locate the middle of the breastbone: for children and infants you will press on the middle of the breastbone; on adults you will press on the lower half of the breastbone.

Turn the person onto their back on a solid surface. For *adults*, place the heel of your hand on the lower half of the breastbone, keeping your fingers parallel to the ribs but relaxed and raised. With your other hand grip the wrist of the first. Get close enough so that your shoulder is directly above the breastbone, then use the weight of your body to press down through your straight arm to the heel of your hand and onto the breastbone. Aim for even, regular pressure and relaxation, compressing the breastbone 4 or 5 cm, with sixty compression per minute at a *rate* of four every three seconds. This allows for eight inflations of the lungs per minute (see *Heart and lungs* above for sequence).

For infants under one year of age, use two fingers only on the middle of the breastbone and compress only 1.5 cm. For children between one and eight, use one hand only just below the middle of the breastbone and compress only 2.5 cm. The rate should be ninety compressions per minute (see *Heart and lungs* and *Summary* above for sequences).

Coma position

This position is sometimes called the lateral recovery position. The person lies on their left side with their left arm extended, their right arm bent over it, their right leg extended at right angles from the body and bent at the knee, and the left leg lying straight. The head should be tilted back to keep the airway open, with the face turned slightly towards the ground so that vomit or other matter can drain from the mouth. Support the jaw.

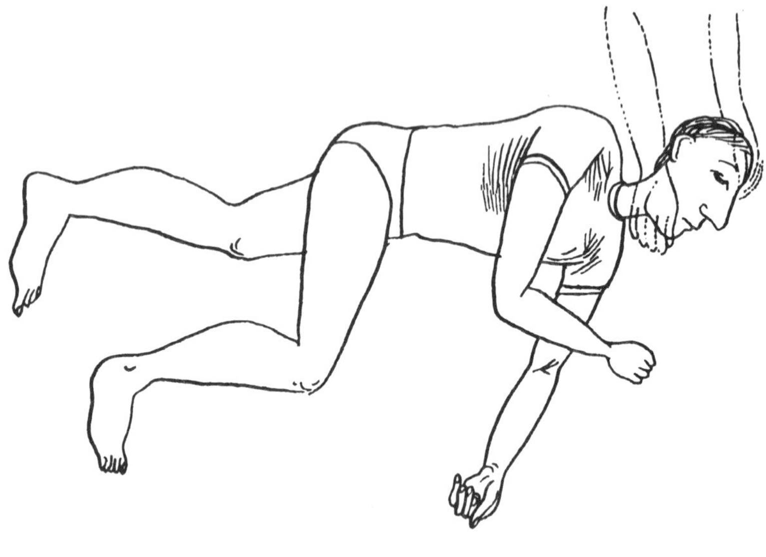

If the person has broken bones that prevent you placing them in this position, support and stabilise them with a rolled blanket or something similar.

Keep checking the person's condition, breathing and heart beat. *Listen* for breaths, *look* for the chest rising and falling, *feel* for the rising chest or expelled breath if visibility is poor and *feel* for the pulse.

Keep the person warm, but make sure you can still check that they are breathing and their heart is beating.

Bleeding

Serious bleeding can be deadly. An adult can afford to loose 500 ml of their 9-11 litres of blood; the loss of 1 litre will cause faintness, 1.5 litres will cause collapse, and a loss of more than 2.25 litres can cause death. Signs of excessive blood loss include pale, cold, clammy skin; a fast weak pulse; giddiness or fainting, blurred vision; thirst or breathlessness; anxiety or talkativeness.

If a lot of blood has been lost or the blood is bright red and spurting (arterial), or bleeding is prolonged, act quickly to stop it. Apply pressure over the wound (unless there is a broken bone beneath), ideally with a sterile dressing, but if there is no clean cloth available, just use your hand. Raise a wounded limb above the level of the heart, and pull together the sides of a gaping wound. Maintain pressure for 5-15 minutes to allow clots to form.

If there is a foreign body in the wound, do not remove it but apply pressure beside it. When bandaging such a wound, build up bulky dressings around the object until you can bandage over it without pressing on it.

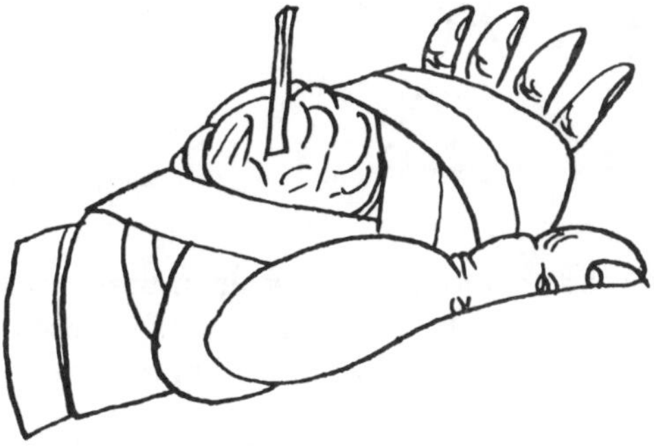

Bandage around a foreign body.

Pressure points

This method should only be used if it is impossible to stop the bleeding by applying pressure to the wound. If the wound is extensive and bleeding very severe, you may have no other alternative, but remember that you will be cutting off the blood supply to an entire limb, so do this as a last resort and for no longer than fifteen minutes at a time.

The two main points used to control arterial bleeding in the arm and leg are in the under side of the upper arm and in the groin. Feel between the muscles on the inside of the upper arm till you feel a pulse then press the artery back against the bone. Check the wound to make sure that the bleeding slows. For leg wounds, bend the person's knee and feel in the fold of the groin round about the centre till you feel a pulse then press it against the pelvis with the heel of your hand.

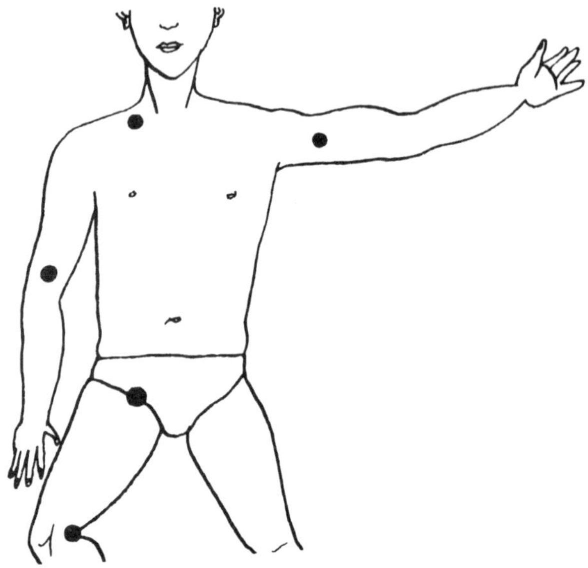

For wounds to the shoulder or upper arm, press midway along the collarbone. For wounds in the lower arm, apply pressure to the crook of the elbow, and for those on the hand, apply pressure to the front (thumb side) of the wrist.

Wounds on the lower leg can be treated with pressure above the back of the knee and those to the foot with pressure on the front of the ankle.

Tourniquets

Use a broad strip of material or bandage (at least 5 cm wide) and tie it firmly around the upper arm or the upper leg depending on the position of the wound. Do not tie it around the lower parts of limbs (the bones prevent adequate pressure being applied to the blood vessels) or the joints. There should be no pulse below the tourniquet and bleeding should decrease. If it does not, or if the person complains of intense pain from the tourniquet, remove it and reposition it properly. To avoid pain, try a wider tourniquet or apply it more loosely.

Take note of the time the tourniquet was applied and get the person to hospital quickly, making sure that everyone knows the tourniquet is in place (it should be visible at all times).

Severe wounds

Head wounds

These are likely to render the person unconscious, in which case they should be placed in the coma position (unless you suspect spinal injury), making sure the airway is open and bleeding is controlled.

Chest wounds

If the wound makes a sucking sound, the chest cavity has been pierced. Cover the wound with the palm of your hand to keep air from entering it and lay the injured person down so that they are leaning towards the injured side with their head and shoulders supported. Cover the wound with cling film or even aluminium foil or plug it with loose dressings that have been wet with boiled water then bandage firmly.

Abdominal wounds

If the gut or some other organ extrudes, do not touch it or try to replace it. Cover the wound with a dressing wet with boiled water and keep it damp. If there is no extruding organ, dress the wound and bandage it firmly. *Do not* give any food or drink. Moisten lips and tongue with a damp cloth or sponge if necessary.

Less severe wounds

If you are far from help, you will have to treat wounds yourself and keep them free from infection. Use soap and boiled water to wash your hands and wounds. Clean from the inside of the wound out. If you cannot boil water, then urine is sterile and can be used to clean wounds. Dry the wound and apply a clean dressing, immobilising the injured part if it gives comfort.

If the dressing becomes smelly or wet, or if the wound throbs or becomes more painful, remove the dressing. Examine for signs of infection (swelling, redness, heat, faint trails of red on the inside of arms or legs, pus, increased pain; if severe, fever, sweating, thirst and lethargy). Treat any infection and replace with a clean dressing. Hot salty water is good for infections, and a poultice of anything that can be mashed should be applied. Boil it up, wrap it in cloth, and apply it hot (but not scalding) to the wound to draw out pus. Even clay will work.

Internal bleeding

Internal bleeding can result from injury or from conditions such as a stomach ulcer; it is just as serious as external bleeding. If a person has been injured or received a blow, or has suffered from a medical condition that could result in internal bleeding, suspect it if you notice any of the following signs: shock, shallow breathing, yawning or sighing; thirst; restlessness or talkativeness; pain or discomfort, swelling, etc., around the affected part; blood from one of the body's orifices.

The type of blood and the orifice can indicate the nature of the injury.

If the *ear* bleeds fresh blood, the eardrum could be perforated; if there is only a little blood mixed with clear fluid from either the *ear* or the *nose* it could be from a fractured skull. If the *nose* loses a lot of fresh blood, it could be broken.

A little fresh blood from the *mouth* could mean a broken jaw; vomited blood that looks like coffee grounds (the blood has been affected by digestive juices) could mean a bleeding ulcer; fresh blood coughed up could mean an injury to the airway, whereas fresh frothy blood indicates lung injury, probably from broken ribs.

If *urine* is blood-stained, the kidneys or bladder could be injured; if the blood is clotted or diluted, the urinary tract or bladder could be injured.

Steady *vaginal* bleeding with cramps probably means severe menstruation, but if the flow is sudden and strong it could be from a miscarriage or abortion.

Fresh blood from the *rectum* is usually from haemorrhoids whereas black digested blood in faeces means bleeding from the small intestine.

Have the person lie down and loosen their clothing. If possible, raise their legs to increase blood flow to the vital organs. Reassure the person and keep them warm. Check for other injuries, and check regularly for breathing, pulse and level of consciousness. Do not allow the person to eat or drink anything, and get medical help as quickly as possible. Place the person in the coma position if they lapse into unconsciousness and see to their airway, breathing and heart beat.

Broken bones

Any of the following signs may indicate a broken bone: pain at the sight of the injury which is more intense with movement; swelling and eventually bruising; difficulty in moving the limb a little or at all; deformity of the limb; a grating sound if the limb is accidentally moved; a crack or snap which the person may have heard.

A closed fracture is one where the skin in not broken; an open fracture is one where the bone protrudes through the skin or is part of an open wound. Infection can enter the bone with open fractures, so be especially careful.

In open fractures, stem bleeding by pressing alongside a bone or by squeezing the sides of the wound together, but do not press down on the wound. Dress the wound and, in the case of a protruding bone, gently build up padding around the bone so that it receives no pressure from bandages. Bandage the wound diagonally so that the bandage does not exert pressure on the underside of the break. Splint, immobilise and support the limb if possible.

The following advice only applies if medical help is unlikely to arrive for many hours, and you are in a true survival situation. You will have to straighten a deformed limb before it is splinted. This is painful, so do it while the person is unconscious if possible. Apply steady traction until the ends of the bone meet or the limb is as straight as the person can bear it to be, then splint and immobilise the limb. Protect the skin with padding. If there is no suitable splint, bind the injured limb to the body or an undamaged limb.

Arm injuries

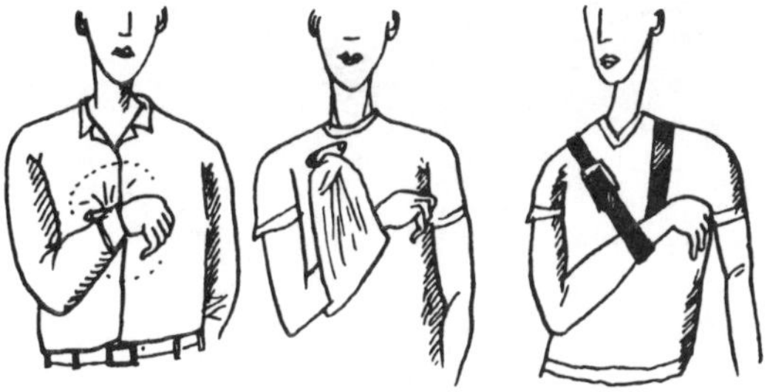

Makeshift slings.

Fractured arm bones, including the collarbone and shoulder blade, should be supported with a sling and splinted where appropriate. The exception is a fractured elbow, where the arm is straight; this should be splinted and strapped to the body, but the arm should not be bent. If after an elbow fracture the arm is bent and there is no pulse, the artery could be blocked by the injury. Gently straighten the arm a little until there is a pulse.

Leg injuries

Fractured leg bones, including hips, should be splinted where possible or the leg should be padded and strapped to the uninjured leg. A broken hip should be supported with a splint to the armpit and another on the inside of the leg. A broken ankle or foot is not usually splinted but should be raised to reduce swelling and immobilised. Do not remove the shoe and sock unless there is an open wound or excessive swelling. Wrap the injury in a pillow or blanket to immobilise it and tie in two or three places, leaving the knots on the outside of the ankle. If there is an open wound, raise the limb and gently remove the shoe and sock. Use pressure to control bleeding and bandage any wounds. To prevent excessive swelling, bandage the ankle and foot. An icepack will help to reduce both pain and swelling.

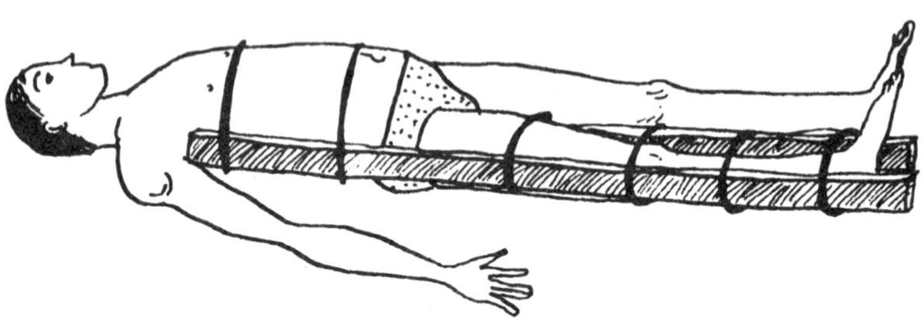

Broken hip.

Fractured pelvis

This will produce pain in the lower abdomen or groin. Place the person on a door or similar flat support and strap them to it (with their knees bent and supported) at the ankles, waist and above the chest, with padding between the thighs and the knees strapped together.

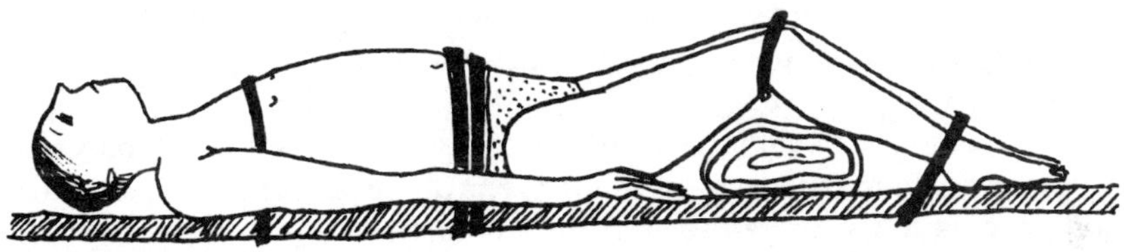

Fractured skull

Check the person's pupils – one may be larger or smaller than the other. Fluid may seep from the nose or an ear.

Lay the person in the coma position with the seeping ear downwards. Cover that ear with a sterile dressing and check pulse and breathing regularly. Keep the person still.

Spinal injury

This is one of the most serious fractures and deserves special treatment because a severed spinal cord produces paralysis.

Checking for spinal injury

Spinal injury can result from a car accident, from whiplash, from diving into shallow water, or falling heavily on the buttocks, head or feet; it can result from something heavy falling on the spine or from a blow. The parts most vulnerable to injury are the neck and the lower back. If you suspect spinal injury because of the nature of the accident or injury, do not move the person unless it is absolutely essential for their survival.

If the person is conscious they may complain about severe back pain or a feeling of being cut in half; they may have lost sensation in limbs or be unable to move their limbs. Without them seeing what you are doing, touch them gently on a limb, working from the extremities inwards and ask if they can feel the touch. Next, ask them to move their fingers and wrists, toes and ankles.

First aid

If the person is unconscious, you must ensure that the airway is clear. Support the head and keep the spine straight (you will need help to do this) as you turn the person onto their side, then follow basic steps for breathing and heartbeat, supporting the person so they do not roll or twist.

Reassure a conscious person and make sure they don't move. If professional help will arrive promptly, simply support the head and feet and prop padding along the body for support.

If professional help is unlikely to arrive promptly, you should steady the person's body and limbs more effectively. While someone holds the shoulders and pelvis, place padding very carefully between the legs, tie a broad bandage round the knees and a figure-of-eight bandage round the ankles and feet.

If the delay is likely to be lengthy, fit a neck collar. Roll a jumper, towel or newspaper to about a 10 cm width and wrap in a triangular bandage, or something similar. With the head and neck supported, place the centre of the collar at the front of the neck, fold both ends round behind and bring them round to the front to tie. Be careful not to obstruct breathing.

Moving a person with spinal-injury

Attempt this only if the person is in very serious danger (this includes suffocation from an obstructed airway). At all costs you must avoid putting any strain on the delicate spinal cord that runs the length of the spine inside the vertebrae. If it is damaged or broken the person could be paralysed from the injury down.

Do not bend or twist the person's back or neck. If possible, have three or four people support the person – the first at the head and neck, the second at the shoulders, the third at the torso, and the fourth at the legs and hips. Lift or roll the person onto a stretcher or blanket

If you are forced to work alone, do not turn the person over unless they are unconscious and the airway is obstructed. If they are face up, pull them out of harm's way by the ankles. If face down, rest the person's head on your forearms and pull them by the shoulders.

Shock

A person can die from shock, so act quickly. Symptoms include weakness, dizziness or faintness; cold clammy skin; weak rapid pulse; thirst; shallow breathing, yawning and sighing; vomiting or unconsciousness; paleness, especially in the lips. Shock can result from severe bleeding, vomiting or diarrhoea; severe burns; electrocution or heart attack.

To treat shock, enough blood must be helped to reach the heart, lungs and brain and the cause of the shock must be discovered and treated. If the person is unconscious, place in the coma position and attend to their airway, breathing and heartbeat. If conscious, reassure the person as you help them to lie down. Raise their legs, if possible, and loosen tight clothing. Treat the cause of the shock and control any bleeding. Keep the person still and warm but not hot. Do not allow them to eat, drink or smoke. Moisten the lips with water if they are thirsty. Check breathing and pulse regularly and get medical help promptly. Be prepared to resuscitate a person if breathing or heartbeat fails. Remain calm and confident, and do not leave the person alone.

Sprains, strains and dislocations

Injuries that are not usually life-threatening can tilt the odds of survival against you if your circumstances are serious enough, so treat all injuries promptly and carefully.

A strain can result from any sudden or violent movement and will produce a sharp pain and possibly swelling. Help the person into a comfortable position and give support to the injury. If a limb is affected, elevate it. If possible, apply an icepack or bathe the injury in cold water.

A sprain is more serious and occurs when the ligaments around a joint are torn. Pain, swelling and later bruising may occur. Treat in the same way as a strain, but after cooling the injury, apply a bandage to give support. If the ankle is sprained and you are far from help, leave the shoe and sock on and bandage over the top of both.

Dislocations occur when a bone is displaced from a joint, most commonly in the jaw, shoulder, elbow, finger or thumb. Pain can be extremely severe and the person will be unable to move the injured part, which may also look deformed. Later the injury will swell and bruising will appear. If you can reach medical assistance, do not try to put back the dislocated bone. Support the injured part with cushions or clothing and immobilise it with a bandage or sling as appropriate. An icepack or cold pack should also be applied.

In extreme conditions where you cannot reach medical help you may have to try to replace the bone in the correct position. Pull a dislocated finger then let it go very gently so that it moves back into position. A thumb is more difficult and should be treated very gently. If it does not work at first, do not repeat the attempt. To replace a dislocated shoulder requires strength. Take off your shoe and place your foot in the person's armpit to brace yourself while you pull on the arm. If you succeed, the person may be more comfortable with their arm supported in a sling or bound to their body. Lastly, to replace a dislocated jaw, place a cloth pad over the lower teeth and support the head firmly with something. Press down on the pad with your thumbs and rotate the dislocated side backwards and upwards. Ideally it should snap into place. It should then be bandaged to give support and only soft foods should be offered.

Bushfire first aid

Firefighting causes many minor ailments that require treatment with a weak saline solution of one part salt to ten parts water. This can be used for bathing sore eyes (it should be boiled and cooled first) and as a gargle for inflamed throats. A weaker solution can be drunk to replace fluid and salts lost through excessive sweating.

Dehydration

Give the person frequent small drinks of plain water (except on medical advice), not one big drink. Cool their body using the method for heat exhaustion. Be alert for symptoms of shock. If no urine or only a very little is passed in twelve hours, get medical attention.

Muscle cramps

These cramps result from salt loss due to excessive sweating. They may be accompanied by dizziness, shallow breathing or even vomiting. These should be taken seriously or heat exhaustion may follow.

Rest in a cool spot. Cramped muscles can be gently stretched and treated with ice packs. Drink water to which a little salt has been added (two pinches or half a teaspoon of salt per litre).

Heat exhaustion

The person looks pale, has cold or clammy skin and feels weak or dizzy, faints or perhaps suffers from cramps, and has a weak or rapid pulse. Rest in a cool spot and drink water to which a little salt has been added. Sponge the person's face, hair and body with cool water and allow it to evaporate.

Heatstroke

This is the most dangerous condition caused by heat. The skin appears flushed and dry and feels hot. *Sweating stops*, the person's temperature rises and their pulse becomes strong and rapid. They may suffer from a severe headache and vomit, finally becoming unconscious.

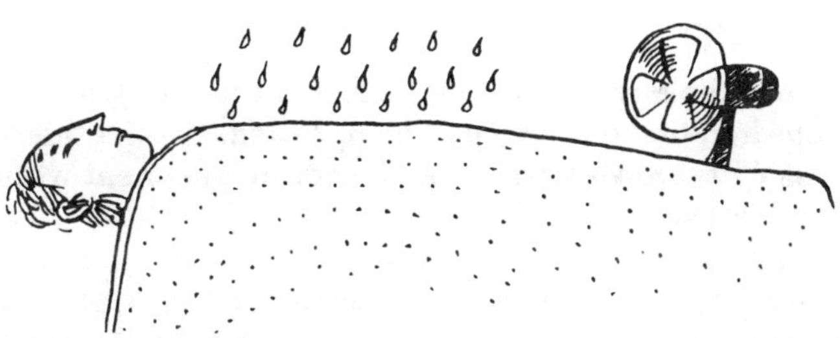

Do not plunge the person into cold water; they may suffer shock. This treatment can only be considered if the alternative is certain death or brain damage. Lay the person in a cool place and remove their clothes, except for their underclothing. Cover them with a wet sheet and fan them to slowly lower the temperature. Continue to sprinkle water and keep air moving over the body. If the person has lapsed into unconsciousness, place them in the coma position. When they are conscious give them water to sip. You may also massage their hands and feet to encourage circulation and heat loss. If the person suddenly becomes cold, cease treatment and cover them with something dry to warm them. If they have been badly affected, you may have to cool them and cover them up more than once until their temperature returns to normal permanently. When the person's temperature returns to normal, replace their clothing. Anyone suffering heatstroke may need urgent medical attention, so be prepared.

Burns

Do not pull clothing off a burn. If clothes must be removed, carefully cut around any that are stuck to a burn.

Immediately treat the burn with cold water or ice. This cools the burn and prevents heat damaging further tissue. You may have to keep cold water running over the burn for some time.

Make sure your hands are very clean before treating someone with burns.

Lie the person down in a comfortable position and reassure them.

Cover burns with a clean dressing. A clean handkerchief or sheet, ironed with a hot iron to destroy microbes, makes a good dressing.

Give something for pain and allow sips of non-alcoholic drink. If the person is badly burned and likely to need surgery, do not give food or it will affect the timing of anaesthesia.

Snake bite

Australia has the most venomous snakes in the world, and each year roughly five hundred people report being bitten. Despite this, very few people die. With proper first aid and medical treatment within eight hours, death is rare.

Symptoms of snake bite occur after 30 to 120 minutes and may include sweating, fainting or drowsiness, vomiting or nausea, diarrhoea, disturbed vision, headache, shock, and finally collapse and respiratory failure. There may or may not be obvious puncture marks.

The Pressure/Immobilisation Method for treating snake bites slows the spread of venom through the circulatory system, allowing the person to survive until medical help arrives. Make sure you warn the hospital or doctor in advance so that treatment can be ready when the person arrives.

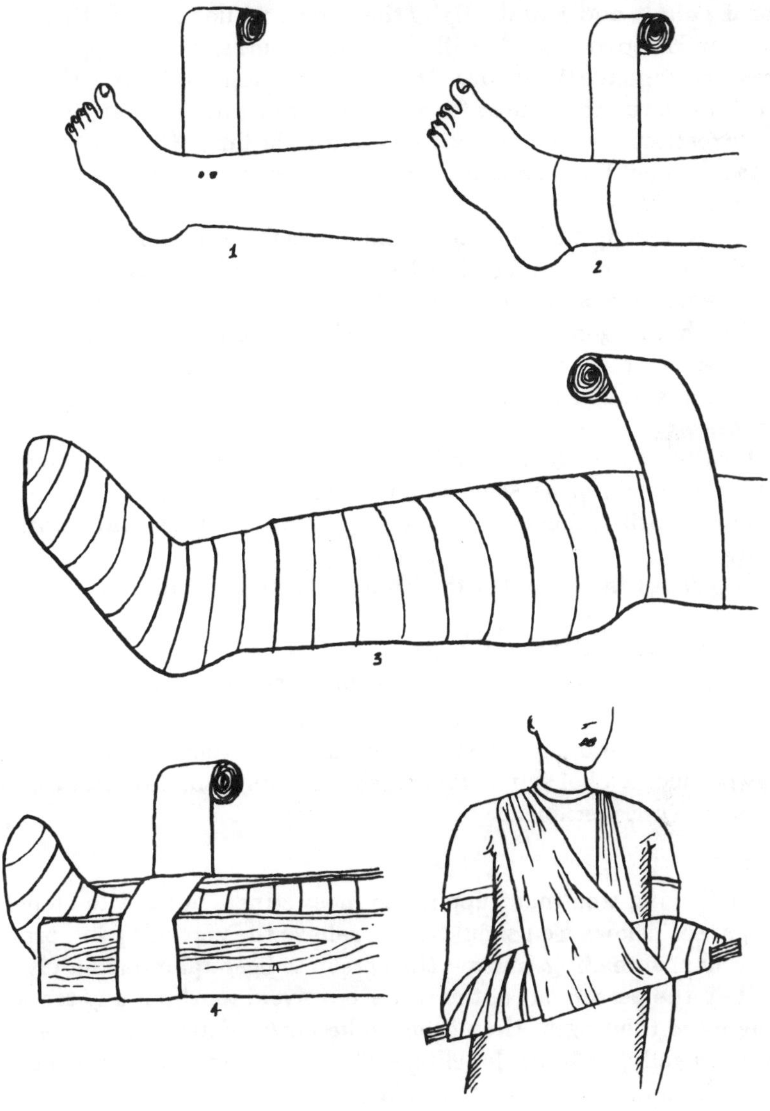

Pressure/Immobilisation Method (PIM).

PIM (Pressure/Immobilisation Method)

Speak calmly and confidently to the person while you help them to lie down and keep completely still. Reassure them regularly. Apply a broad pressure bandage firmly over the bite and extend it down to the end of the limb and up the limb as far as possible towards the heart. Take care not to restrict the flow of blood to the end of the limb. (Check that fingers or toes are not blue, pale, tingling, numb, or very cold, and that there is a pulse.)

Apply a splint to completely immobilise the limb using anything at hand. If the bite is on a foot or leg, bind the splinted leg firmly to the other leg; if it is on an arm or hand, put the splinted arm in a sling.

Watch the general condition of the person and if they become unconscious, place them in the coma position and check their airway, breathing and heartbeat regularly. Be prepared to start resuscitation if necessary.

Ideally, get medical help to the person or if necessary move the person to hospital as soon as possible. The bandage should not be removed until the doctor has the appropriate drugs and treatment ready.

Do not cut the wound or the limb, or apply a tourniquet.

Sea creature stings

See the section on *Dangerous creatures* for detailed treatment for particular creatures. The stung person may suffer intense pain, nausea, vomiting, skin marks, cramps, weakness or paralysis, shock, they may produce a lot of saliva, their breathing may fail, they may collapse or become unconscious.

Treatment

The following treatment applies to most stings, but not to stonefish stings (see below). You should try to relieve the person's pain, prevent the venom spreading, and get the person to hospital immediately.

Help the person out of the water but avoid touching any tentacles clinging to their skin. Help them to lie down. Pour plenty of *vinegar* only onto jellyfish tentacles clinging to the skin to disable them before you pick them off. *Do not use anything else* – the substance could set off further stinging capsules in the tentacles.

Once the tentacles have been de-activated and removed, apply a pressure bandage over the sting and follow the pressure/immobilisation method. Get the person to hospital immediately, keeping a close watch on their condition. If they become unconscious, place them in the coma position and attend to their airway, breathing and heartbeat. Be prepared to start resuscitation if necessary.

Stonefish stings

Pain relief is important. If you cannot reach a doctor quickly, apply water hot enough to bear but not scalding to the wound; this may inactivate and disperse some of the venom, thus reducing the severity of the pain. If there is a severe reaction resuscitation may be necessary.

Effects of heat

Sunburn

If you can't avoid sunburn, rest in the shade, have a cool drink and apply cool water or cloths to reddened skin. Cold tea can be soothing if you do not have sunburn lotion. Do not burst blisters or peel off skin.

Prickly heat

Remove clothing and, if possible, wash in cool water. Allow clothes to dry before putting them on again, but don't risk sunburn.

Muscle cramps

Get out of the sun and rest in a shady spot. Drink water to which a little salt has been added (two pinches of salt per litre).

Heat exhaustion and heatstroke

Rest in a shady spot and drink water to which a little salt has been added. (See *Bushfire first aid* for heatstroke treatment details.)

Effects of cold

Trench foot

To treat trench foot, make sure the feet are dry, but take care not to rub the skin or burst the blisters or massage the feet. Keep them up and make sure they are warm, but do not use a heater or hot water bottle, etc.

Frostbite

If the waxy patches have just appeared, warm them gradually. They will be painful when they have recovered. Remove anything tight that could restrict blood flow.

For deep frostbite, thaw in warm, not hot, water. If this is impossible, warm the victim with your own body. Cover the affected part to prevent injury.

If the frostbite is heated too quickly, there will be intense pain. *Do not* rub the part with snow or anything else, or burst blisters, or heat in front of a fire. Do not try to warm the part by exercising. Do not use force to remove shoes, boots, gloves or mittens that are frozen on. Do not let the person walk on a frostbitten foot.

Thaw in *warm* water.

Snow blindness

Put the person somewhere dark and bandage the eyes to keep out light. Lay a damp cloth on the forehead to keep it cool, and wait for the blindness to correct itself.

Hypothermia

To treat hypothermia, first of all make sure the victim does not lose any more heat. Get them to shelter and wrap some insulating material around them, covering everything but their face. Only then remove any wet clothes one piece at a time, replacing them with dry clothes before the next wet item is removed. Warm gradually with other bodies or warm rocks or water bottles (not hot ones) placed where major blood vessels are close to the skin (armpits, back of the neck, small of the back and pit of the stomach, groin, and between the thighs but not on the extremities). *Do not* rub or massage the limbs or allow the person to exercise – blood will be removed from the vital organs to the extremities. If the victim is conscious, give warm drinks with plenty of sugar and sugary food. *Do not* allow them to sit up or their blood pressure may fall suddenly.

Do not give alcohol or raise the temperature too quickly – if surface blood vessels dilate, heat could be drawn away from vital organs and the victim could die. Even when the temperature is back to normal, the person will not have fully recovered – they will need time before they are out of danger.

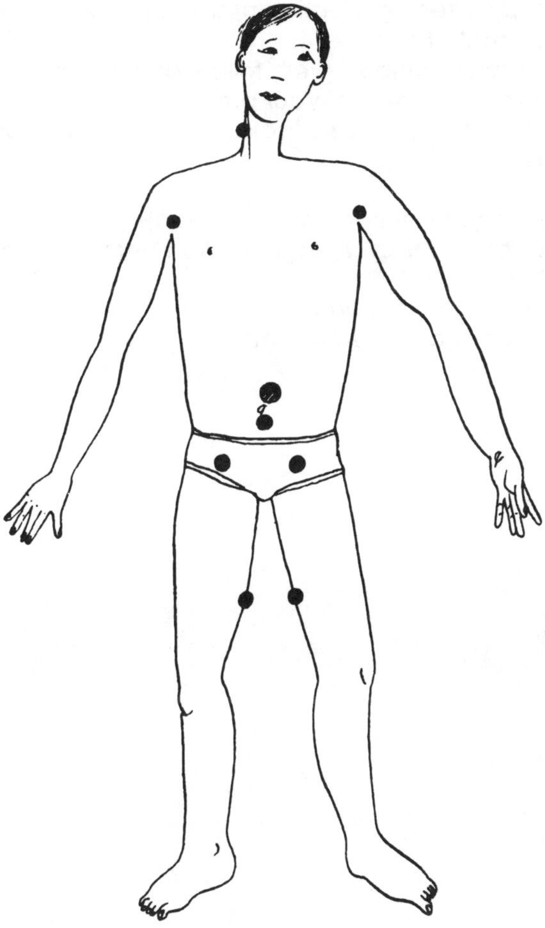

Apply warmth here.

SUMMARY

- ❑ You can survive for many days without food.
- ❑ Avoid fat and protein if water is scarce.
- ❑ Prevent prey seeing, hearing or smelling you.
- ❑ Learn animals' habits.
- ❑ Don't chase wounded prey; follow at a distance.
- ❑ Don't waste any part of your prey.
- ❑ Catch fish on improvised tackle, with traps, explosives or by 'tickling'.
- ❑ Use local bait.
- ❑ Use the edibility test on unknown plants.
- ❑ Know what plants and fungi to avoid before you need them to survive.
- ❑ Insects are rich in fat and protein.
- ❑ Avoid brightly coloured insects.

5 FOOD

Food is less critical to your survival than water and may even be less important than, say, shelter or avoiding extremes of temperature. Nevertheless it is the subject that most people think of first in relation to survival. If you are really hungry, you will be prepared to eat almost anything to survive, and eating almost anything, with some important exceptions, will probably keep you alive until help arrives.

If you have plenty of water but little food, drink more water than usual and exert yourself as little as possible. You can survive for many days without food.

Meat

With the exception of some unusual things such as dog liver, which causes vitamin A poisoning, most freshly-killed meat is safe to eat so long as it is well cooked. If you are short of water, avoid eating too much protein or fat – both take a lot of water from the body during digestion.

Traps and snares

There is a vast array of traps and snares that can be built to catch game and even fish, from simple deadfalls (a rock propped on a stick with bait underneath and a cord attached to the stick) to elaborate traps that hoist game into the air or stab them with stakes.

If help is going to be a very long time coming, you may be forced to trap game. If so, you will have to try to leave as little of your scent on the trap as possible and to camouflage it effectively. Coating your hands with mud will help disguise your scent, especially if you are careful to avoid handling soap, petrol, oil or any other strong-smelling human artefacts. Avoid stepping on the trail or disturbing it in any way. Remember to make your trap too strong rather than not strong enough. Even a rabbit can kick and struggle with great strength and determination when it is caught. Check traps and snares regularly to avoid prey suffering unnecessarily, or escaping, or being taken by other animals.

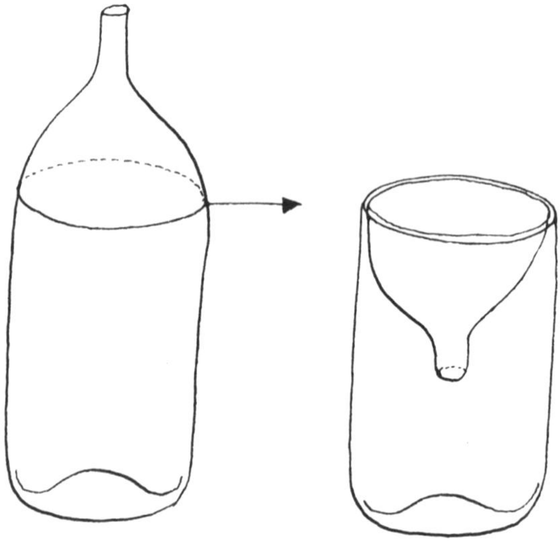

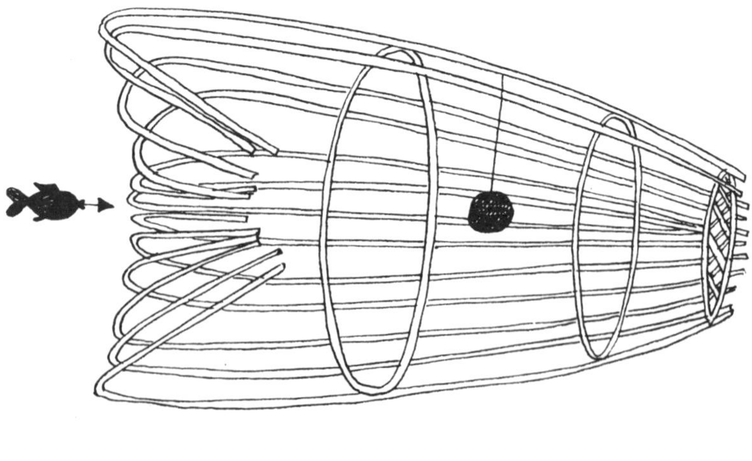

Mammals

Be alert for animal signs such as tracks, fresh droppings, burrows, etc. Many animals follow the same tracks each day, so set up traps and snares along well-frequented tracks. If you can find a burrow (always taking care to check for snakes first) you can see if anything is inside by pushing a long stick with a frayed end or a twisted piece of wire into the burrow and twirling it when you reach the end. If it comes out with fur on it, you can proceed; if not, try another burrow. Sometimes if you twist and push hard enough you can entangle enough fur to drag the animal out of the burrow. If you have enough nets (they should have a running loop at the circumference) to cover all the holes of a warren, you can peg them out then try to smoke out the rabbits or other animals by setting a fire in one of the holes and piling on green foliage. It is also possible to dig out a burrow, but weigh up the amount of energy you will expend against your possible catch.

Some basic hunting rules are worth remembering.

- ❑ Think about when and where animals are likely to gather. They will come to drink, often at the same place, and they will often

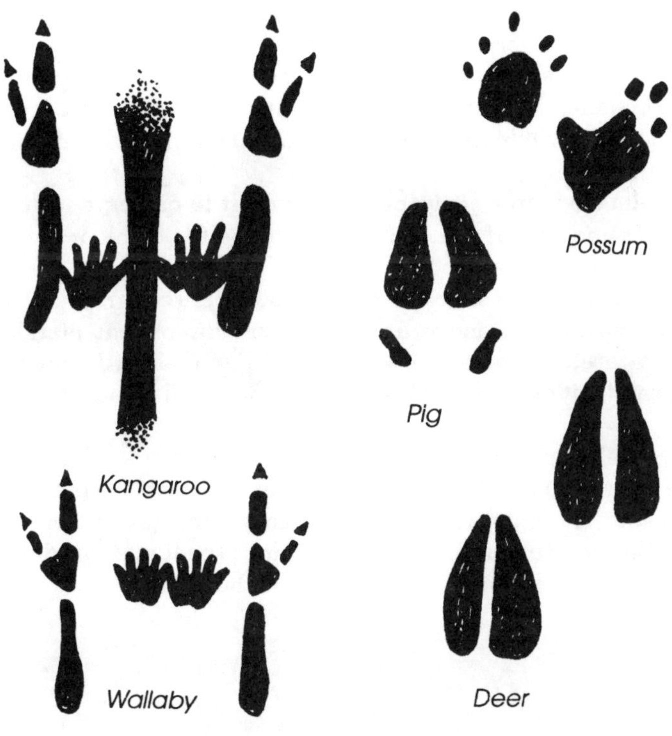

be active at night or at dawn and dusk. If they follow a track one day they will probably use it the next.

- Do not get downwind of the animal or it will pick up your scent.
- Make yourself difficult to see by keeping off the skyline and keeping the sun behind you. If you can camouflage yourself, so much the better.
- Be silent. Avoid standing on sticks or shouldering through dense undergrowth. If an animal seems to sense you presence, keep still until it returns to what it was doing. If you freeze you will be harder to see.
- If an animal is wounded, don't follow it immediately. Keep well back and follow the trail of blood until it weakens. If you frighten it, it could take off and travel kilometres at speed before it finally collapses.
- Aim for the head or neck if your aim is true, or just behind the shoulders where the heart lies if you are less confident. Do not attack hastily or you may frighten off everything in the vicinity.

Killing and butchering game

If you do not feel confident about killing a large trapped animal, you can, if you must, stab it in the neck. Use your knife tied firmly to a long stick to make a spear. The animal will weaken from loss of blood, and you can then come close enough to club it hard on the head.

Once the animal is unconscious or dead, quickly cut the main blood vessels by cutting beneath the jaw and up behind the ears. Hang the animal so that it will bleed as freely as possible. This will help the meat to keep.

Catch the blood in a container and cover it to preserve it. It is rich in nutrients and salt. If you can't bring yourself to drink or eat it raw, cook it or add it to other food.

Before the animal cools, skin it, being careful to cut around the anus and genitals and to remove any strong-smelling scent glands. Cut deeply and carefully round the anus and pull out a length of rectum so that you can tie it off and prevent the contents spilling out and spoiling the meat.

Slit the belly open, using your fingers on either side of the knife as a guide so that you don't cut too deeply and puncture the intestines or other organs. The guts will protrude through the slit and can be cut free. Cut through the diaphragm and remove the lungs, windpipe and heart. Remove the kidneys and liver. Joint the meat.

Almost every part of most animals can be used so long as you are careful to avoid diseased tissue. Look for growths, enlarged or discoloured lymph glands, mottled or black and white spotted lungs or liver, ulcers, etc., and discard the organ or the meat surrounding the diseased part. The blood, stomach (and even its contents in some animals), lungs, kidneys, liver (remove the bile bladder first), pancreas, heart, intestines as well as the head, tail, feet and bones can all be used. If rescue is likely to be a long time coming, do not waste anything.

Cook and eat the offal promptly. The muscle meat can be hung in a place out of reach of other animals and birds or better still sliced thinly and set out to dry in hot, dry weather. If you are fortunate enough to have a supply of salt, meat can be kept in a strong salt solution or cut into pieces and packed in salt. Only use salt if you have a secure and plentiful supply of drinking water. Keep fat for eating or for slush lamps, using a twist of rag for a wick.

Fish

If you are by the sea, there is probably a wide variety of native foods: crabs; molluscs such as periwinkles, mussels, oysters, etc. on rocks or buried in sand; seaweeds; and fish (if you have a hook and line in your emergency kit). Check tide pools carefully – they may contain small fish and there will almost certainly be crabs.

Plants such as pigface or purslane may also be found growing on the shore. Test seaweeds using the edibility test below before eating in any quantity.

In fresh water you may also find molluscs, as well as yabbies or fresh-water crayfish and fish. Certain water plants such as bulrushes (young white shoots) and watercress can also be gathered.

If you do not have fishing line and hook, improvise with thorns, natural twines, bones, etc. Consider creating a fish trap from materials at hand, or fish spears. If you have a gun, you can fire into the water (keep the barrel well clear of the water though) and stun or kill fish, and explosives will do the same, as well as driving fish to the surface at some distance from the blast where they can be collected. If you have the materials and time you can create a strong net to string across a stream or use as a trap or scoop.

It is possible to catch trout by 'tickling' them. Slide your hand quietly into the water behind a fish that is close to the bank and rub the side of the fish gently, working towards the gills. Once you have reached the gills, grab the fish and flip it out onto the bank.

Search for live bait or plants along the edge of the water – fish are most likely to take something local and recognisable. If you are unsuccessful during the day, set night lines with numbers of hooks along a line or set out fish traps.

Most fish traps are based on one idea – fish or other water creatures can enter the trap through a narrow opening after bait or simply by moving with the current; they are then unable to escape, either because the current is against them or the opening is too small for them to negotiate from that direction.

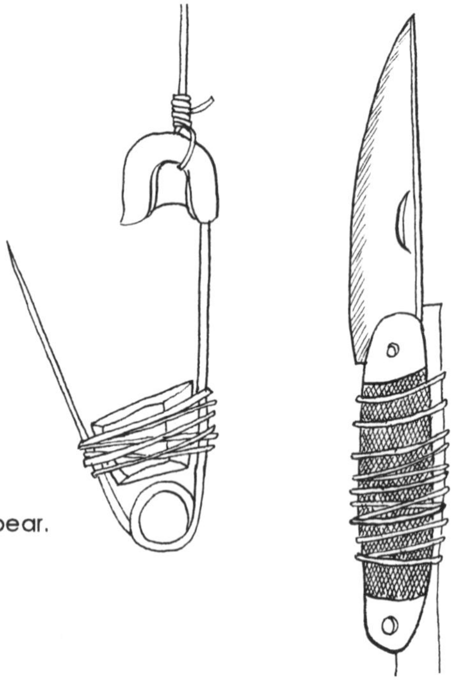

Makeshift hook and spear.

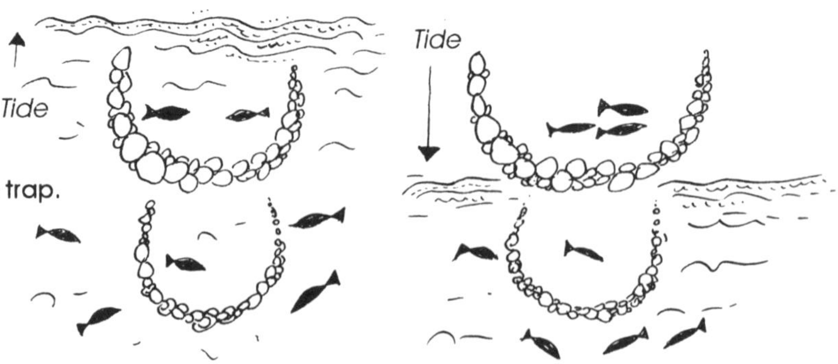

Fish trap.

Reptiles

Snakes, lizards and turtles can be eaten once the heads, guts and skins have been removed, and, of course, the shell in the case of turtles. Take great care when trying to catch a snake – you will die much faster from snake bite than you will from starvation. Choose a springy green stick to beat a snake to death; a dry branch will break. Do not grab a snake by the tail, even if it is disappearing into a hole.

If you can find a stick with a shallow fork at one end, use it to pin a reptile to the ground just behind the head while you club it on the head with a heavy stick.

Birds

Even unappealing birds such as crows can be eaten safely. Birds can be trapped under deadfalls or in nets or snares. Place these where birds habitually fly or land for water or food.

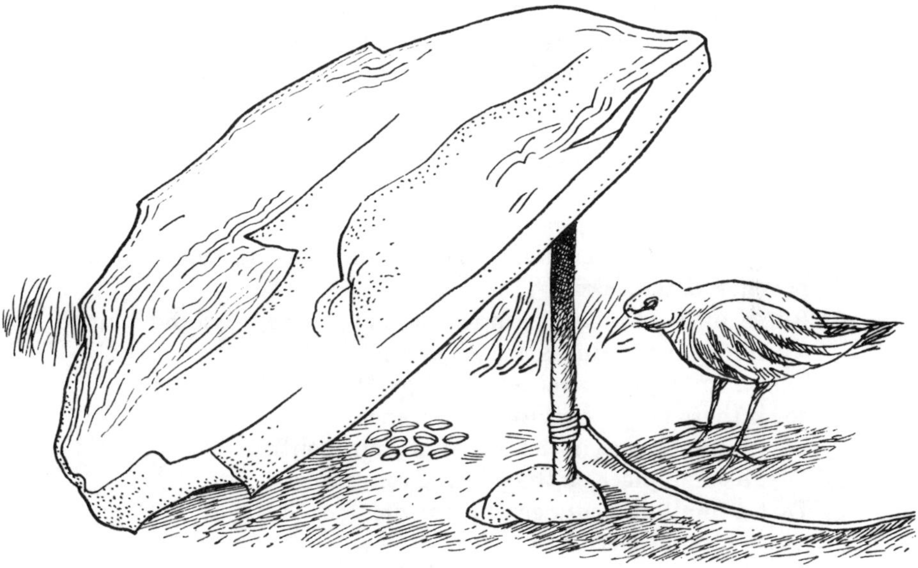

Deadfall.

Once caught and killed, birds should be bled and gutted, and the larger ones skinned. It is probably easiest to burn off feathers rather than pluck them. If you can locate nesting birds then you may have a

supply of eggs or fledglings, but before you put your hand into a nest, check for snakes who may have the same idea.

Amphibians

With the exception of the introduced cane toad and possibly native toads which are or could be poisonous, the legs of most frogs are probably safe to eat once they have been skinned. To kill a frog, drive a knife or sharp stick into the neck just behind the head.

Plants

Certain fungi, seeds and grains, as well as other parts of plants, can contain deadly poisons. Test seeds and grains using the test below, but do not swallow. Any seed that tastes bitter or unpleasant, or has a hot taste, should be rejected. If you are gathering grass seeds, beware of black spurs or bean-like 'grains' replacing the normal seeds. They contain the poisonous ergot fungus, which can also infect grains such as rye.

Elaborate processing can make certain plant foods safe, but simple cooking may not be sufficient; for example, it will *not* destroy the poisonous substances in fungi.

Edibility test

If you are not sure whether part of a plant is safe to eat, test it as follows, waiting at least half a minute for any ill effects.

- ❑ Choose a healthy specimen.
- ❑ Crush and smell a small piece. If it smells of bitter almonds or peaches, don't risk it.
- ❑ Rub a little on tender skin (inside upper arm, say) and wait to see if it causes redness, a rash or blisters.
- ❑ Test a small piece against your lips. Wait half a minute or so to see if there is any irritation or soreness.
- ❑ Test a small piece in the corner of your mouth.
- ❑ Test a small piece on the point of your tongue.
- ❑ Test a small piece under your tongue.
- ❑ Chew a small piece.
- ❑ Swallow a small piece and wait five hours without eating or drinking anything else that could influence your response.
- ❑ If you are still uncertain, continue to test at five-hour intervals for up to eighteen hours. If there is still no reaction, that *part* of the plant is probably safe.

Should you have any adverse reactions, there are several things you can do. If you fear poisoning, try to vomit by sticking a finger down your throat or swallowing some charcoal. To relieve stomach pain drink plenty of hot (clean!) water or take some white wood ash mixed to a paste with water.

Describing a range of edible plants from the broad range of habitats in Australia and neighbouring islands is beyond the scope of this book. Specialist texts are available on the subject. However there are a number of rules of thumb that are worth memorising when selecting unknown plants to eat. These plants should be rejected:

- ❑ Old or withered leaves may develop poisons as they wilt.
- ❑ Unknown red plants.
- ❑ Plants with milky sap, unless they are well-known, such as figs or dandelions.
- ❑ Plants with barbs or hairs on stems and leaves can cause irritations.
- ❑ Fruit with five segments.
- ❑ Mature bracken breaks down vitamin B in the body. The tightly curled growing heads are edible.
- ❑ Plants that smell of bitter almonds or peaches.
- ❑ Plants that produce a stinging or burning sensation on the skin or tongue.

Fungi

Certain fungi are deadly poisonous, and others will make you ill. In fact, if there are any other types of food available to you, avoid fungi – it is not worth the risk. Even a small amount can be deadly. If you have no alternative, watch for the following signs and discard the fungi:

- ❑ Cup or volva, at or near the base of the stem or stem ring. Dig up the mushroom to check.
- ❑ Gilled button mushrooms are too difficult to identify – discard them.
- ❑ Mushrooms with pale or milky juice.
- ❑ Phosphorescent fungi (check after dark).
- ❑ Yellow or orange fungi growing on wood, or those with overlapping convex caps on solid stems.
- ❑ Fungi with white gills and smooth, flat red top.
- ❑ Fungi with small reddish pores under the cups or red anywhere else.
- ❑ Fungi that turn blue or yellow when bruised.
- ❑ Overripe, decaying or maggotty fungi.

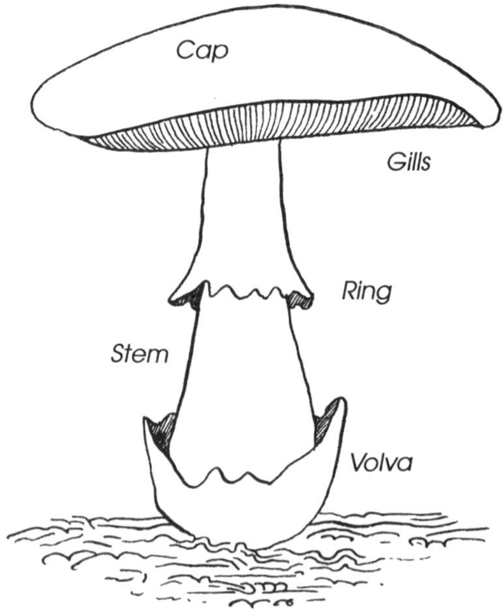

Young puffballs are edible while the insides are still white; the common field mushrooms are also edible, so long as they do not turn yellow when bruised. These are commonly white, fawn or brown on top with gills anything between fawny pink through dark brown to black. There should be no cup at the base of the stem, and any button mushrooms should be treated with great caution because of the difficulty of identifying them. If they are clearly part of a ring of field mushrooms and there are no other varieties of fungus nearby, they are probably safe. Other varieties are also edible, but it is better to gain first-hand knowledge of these (before you ever need to use them) from a reputable source rather than relying on descriptions in books.

Insects

Don't forget insects; they often are rich in fat, protein and carbohydrate. Avoid any that are brightly coloured – this is often nature's way of warning that they are poisonous. Those feeding on carrion or dung may carry infection, although maggots can be eaten if you are hungry enough.

Of the edible insects, witchetty grubs come to mind at once, but the larvae of ants can also be eaten (throw them into water to free them of dirt). Ants themselves can be eaten so long as they are cooked for more than five minutes to destroy any poison. Hunt for ants and grubs in tree trunks or roots or stumps. Bogong moths, cicadas, grasshoppers, even march flies can be eaten, and bush bees may lead you to honey. Bees themselves can be eaten, but remove the sting, wings and legs. Large numbers of small insects can be ground into a paste and added to a soup or stew to increase its nutrients.

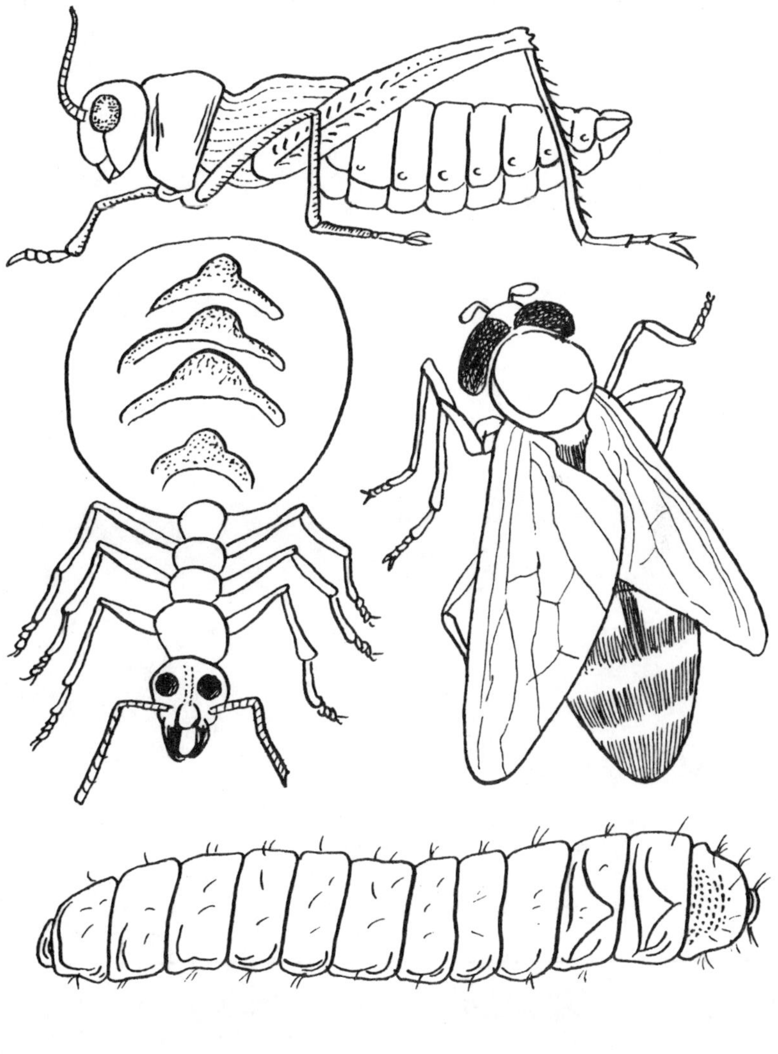

SUMMARY

- ❑ Learn about a region's weather from:
  - weather maps
  - long-range forecasts
  - tourist information
  - local experts
- ❑ Learn to predict weather from clouds, winds and other signs.

6 WEATHER MAPS & SIGNS

Avoiding bad weather can be the most important factor in a person's survival. If you are planning to go into the bush or the mountains, out to sea or even along the coast, make sure you find out as much as possible about local weather conditions beforehand. The weather bureau, especially one that can provide long-range forecasts; local experts such as farmers, or staff at state or national parks; tourist information; or reliable guide books can all give you information about local conditions and the range of weather you are likely to meet.

Weather maps

Make sure you know how to read a weather map and take note of them for at least a week or so before you leave so you can be aware of temperature extremes and of any developments or trends in the weather.

Pressure systems move across the continent generally from west to east. A *high* pressure system usually means fine, calm weather; a *low* pressure system can mean rain or cold unsettled weather.

A *cold* or *warm front* is found where high and low pressure systems meet. Cold fronts bring a cool or cold change, warm fronts the reverse. When a cold front meets warm moist air, the cold air forces it upwards where it condenses into clouds and, probably, rain. If the warm air is unstable, thunderstorms may result. When a warm front meets cooler air, it is forced up over the cool air and again, if there is enough moisture in the warm air, it will condense into rain.

Isobars (the lines on the map) are a little like contour lines on a topographical map, except they join points of equal atmospheric pressure. If the isobars are close together, the winds will be strong; if they are far apart, the winds will be moderate or non-existent. Winds blow clockwise and slightly inwards in a low pressure system and anti-clockwise and slightly outwards in a high, in other words, parallel to the isobars.

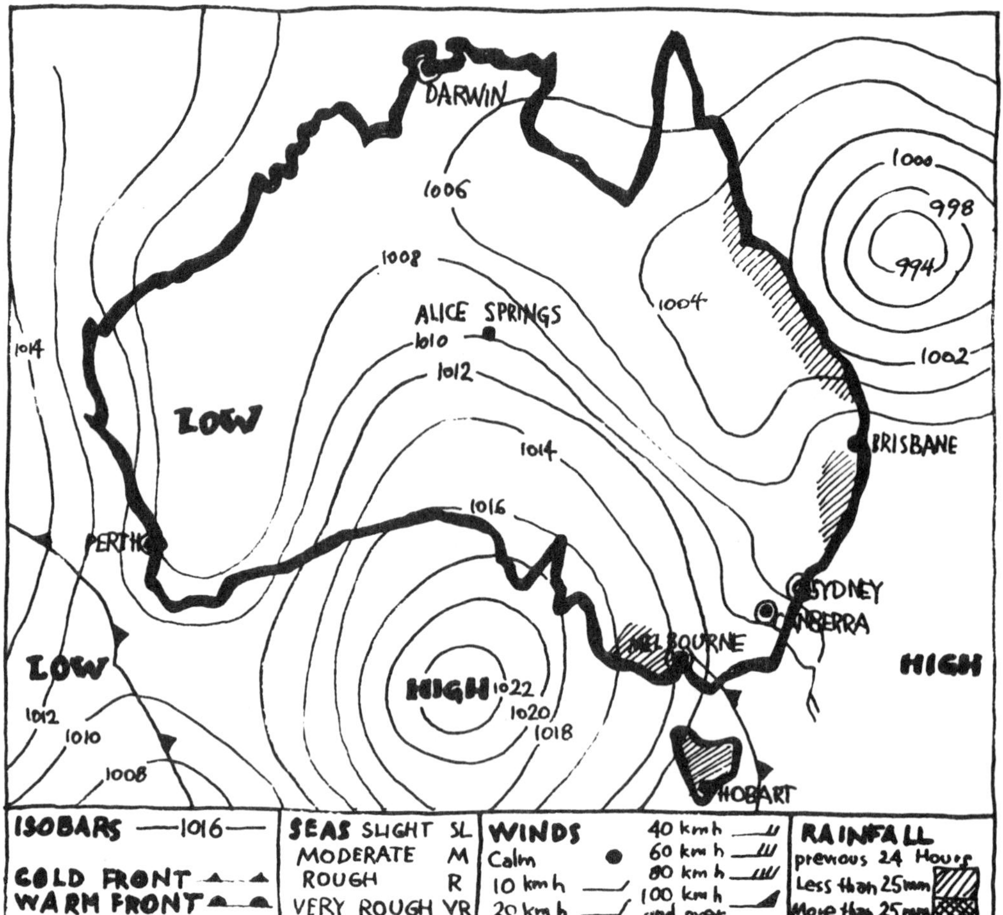
DARWIN
1006
1000
998
994
1008
1004
ALICE SPRINGS
1014
1010
1012
1002
LOW
1014
BRISBANE
1016
PERTH
SYDNEY
CANBERRA
MELBOURNE
LOW
HIGH
HIGH
1022
1012
1020
1010
1018
1008
HOBART
ISOBARS —1016—
COLD FRONT
WARM FRONT
SEAS SLIGHT SL
MODERATE M
ROUGH R
VERY ROUGH VR
WINDS
Calm
10 km h
20 km h
40 km h
60 km h
80 km h
100 km h and over
RAINFALL
previous 24 Hours
Less than 25mm
More than 25mm

Weather signs

All signs fail in a drought.

Despite this saying, it is useful to know a little about the signs that presage weather changes and what they might mean, especially if you suddenly find yourself in danger because of some mishap, without the benefit of weather maps or expert advice.

Winds

A sudden increase in wind strength on a fine day means that bad weather may be blowing in. Fog and mist will not usually be followed by rain unless a wind rises and blows them away. On the other hand, a strong steady dry wind means unchanging weather unless it drops or swings round to another direction, in which case rain may follow.

Clouds

Clouds are usually divided into three categories: high, medium and low. High clouds include *cirrus* (thin wispy 'mare's tails'), *cirrostratus* (thin high veil forming a halo round the sun or moon) and *cirrocumulus* ('mackerel sky', like sand ripples; they warn of weather changes to come. For example, high winds and cirrus clouds usually mean bad weather is on the way; cirrocumulus often follow a storm and give way to clear skies; darkening cirrostratus clouds can presage rain or snow.

Middle clouds include *altocumulus* (high cotton-wool rolls, often after a storm) and *altostratus* (thin sheets or mass of cloud, often thickening and becoming grey and sombre just before rain).

Low clouds include *cumulus* (fluffy and white) and *stratocumulus* (layers of cumulus) both of which usually mean fine weather, unless the cumulus are large with many heads, in which case heavy showers could be on the way. Cumulus clouds at sea in an otherwise cloudless sky may indicate the presence of land. The rain clouds include *stratus* (very low clouds that can bring drizzle), *nimbostratus* (dark low mass leading to continuous or heavy rain or snow) and *cumulonimbus* (thunder clouds, often with an anvil top, bringing storms with hail or winds or thunder and lightning).

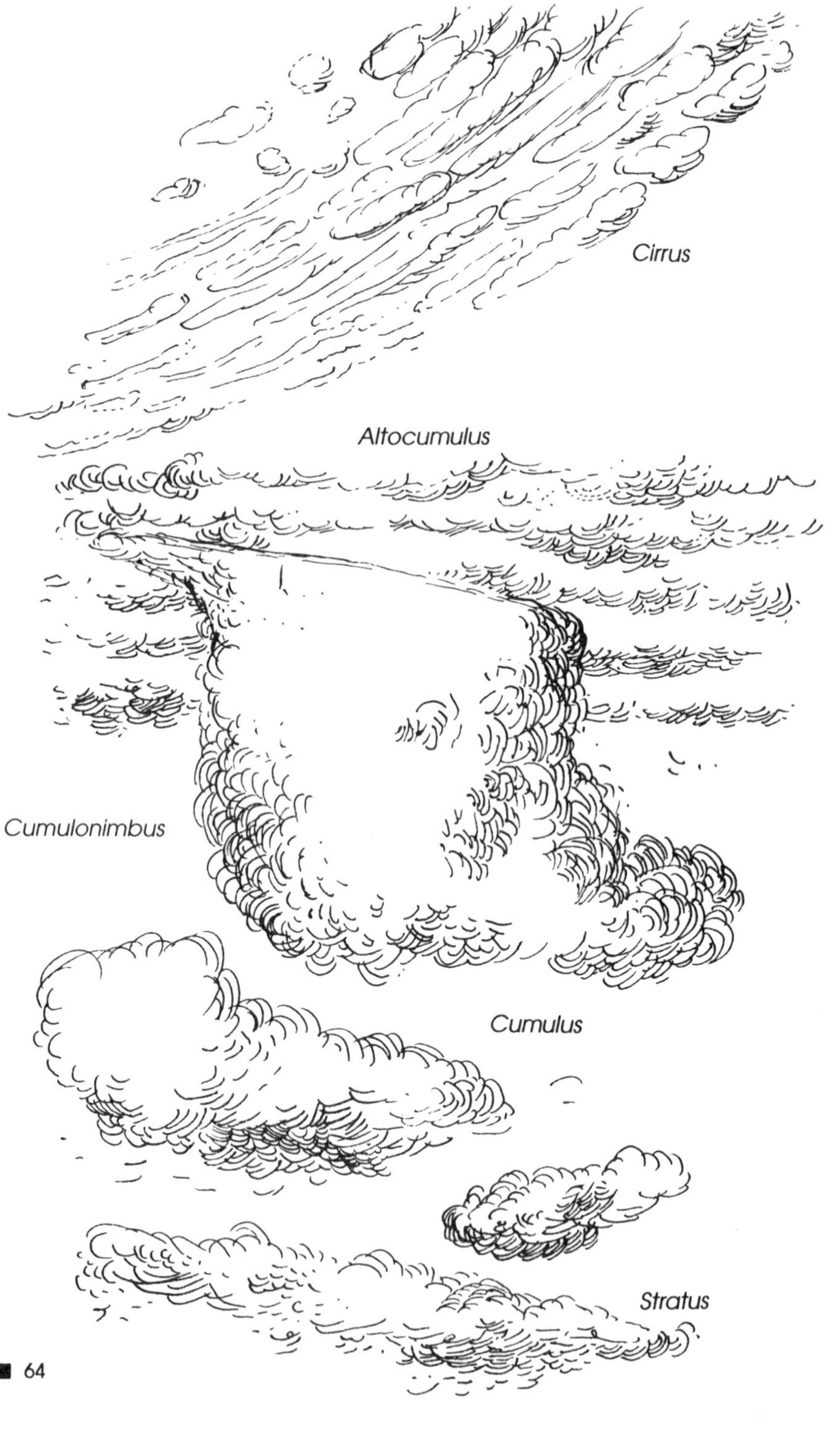
Cirrus
Altocumulus
Cumulonimbus
Cumulus
Stratus

Other signs

Red sky at night – shepherds' delight,
Red sky in the morning – shepherds' warning.

Swifts, in particular the white-throated needletail, mostly feed ahead of a change in the weather, often before summer thunder storms where rising warm humid air brings out insects. They are also attracted to bushfires, where they feed amongst the smoke. Other insect-eating birds will feed high in good weather and low when a storm is on the way.

Ants will become more active before rain, sometimes moving eggs to higher ground, and if you notice rodents are unusually active, especially during the day, it could also mean bad weather. There are other signs that rain is on the way: sounds carry further; hills appear to be closer; vegetation smells are easier to detect; a chimney will smell of soot; curly hair curls more tightly and becomes unruly; old injuries, rheumatic joints or bones ache and corns are uncomfortable; a corona round the sun or moon will shrink; the sky will become grey at evening or duck-egg blue; small scattered clouds appear at evening in an otherwise clear sky; or a rainbow will appear in the morning. The pallid cuckoo or rain bird's call (a rising series of notes) is said to warn of rain.

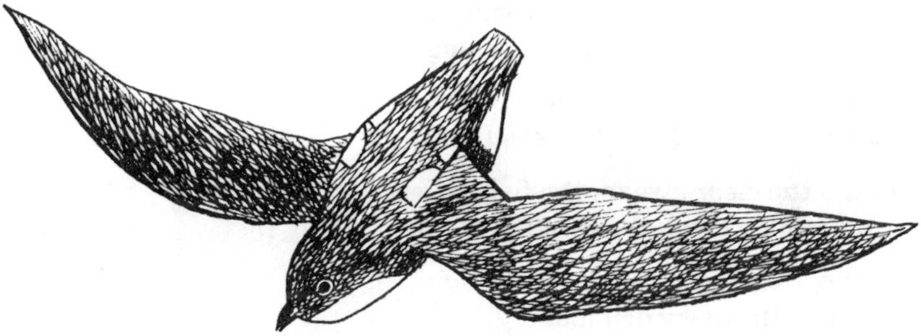

Signs of fine weather are less numerous: a red sky at night; an enlarged corona around the sun or moon; a rainbow late in the afternoon; smoke from a fire rising steadily.

Storms are indicated by a red sky in the morning and smoke from a fire failing to rise more than a short distance. Dust will also hang low in the air if rough weather is on the way.

Edward Jenner, the man who developed vaccination, collected many of the signs of rain in England and put them into his poem of that name.

Signs of rain

The hollow winds begin to blow:
The clouds look black; the glass is low;

The soot falls down; the spaniels sleep;
And spiders from their cobwebs creep.

Last night, the sun went pale to bed;
The moon in halos hid her head.

The boding shepherd heaves a sigh,
For, see, a rainbow spans the sky.

The walls are damp; the ditches smell;
Closed is the pink-eyed pimpernel.

Hark how the chairs and table crack!
Old Betty's bones are on the rack.

Loud quack the ducks; the peacocks cry;
The distant hills are looking nigh.

How restless are the snorting swine!
The busy flies disturb the kine.

Low o'er the grass the swallow wings;
The cricket, too, how sharp he sings.

Puss, on the hearth, with velvet paws,
Sits wiping o'er her whiskered jaws.

Through the clear stream the fishes rise,
And nimbly catch the incautious flies.

The glow-worms, numerous and bright,
Illumed the dewy dell last night.

At dusk, the squalid toad was seen,
Hopping and crawling o'er the green.

The whirling wind the dust obeys,
And in the rapid eddy plays.

The frog has changed his yellow vest,
And in a russet coat is drest.

My dog, so altered in his taste,
    Quits mutton bones, on grass to feast.

And see yon rooks, how odd their flight –
    They imitate the gliding kite,

And headlong downward seem to fall
    As if they felt the piercing ball.

'Twill surely rain: I see with sorrow,
    Our jaunt must be put off to-morrow.

Edward Jenner

If you are good at memorising poetry, you will be able to carry this list of signs around in your head, although pimpernels and peacocks may be in short supply if you are lost in the bush.

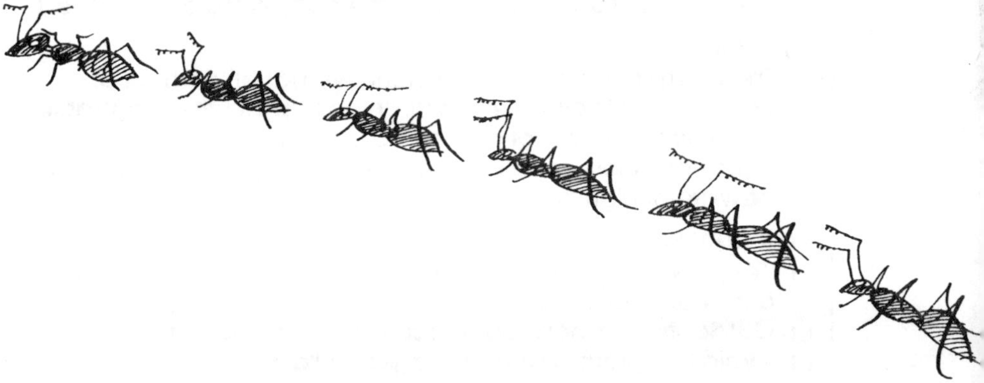

SUMMARY

Fire

- ❑ Fire kills with radiant heat; cover up and find solid shelter.
- ❑ Fire travels fast, especially up hill; you can't outrun it.
- ❑ The fire front will pass in several minutes.
- ❑ Don't run or drive into smoke or flame.
- ❑ Stay in your vehicle – it's safer.
- ❑ Panic will exhaust and muddle you; if you catch fire, stop, drop and roll.
- ❑ Do not shelter in above-ground tanks.

Floods

- ❑ Avoid low-lying areas and dry creek beds.
- ❑ Never enter flood waters; they are dangerous and polluted.

Cyclones

- ❑ The calm at the eye of a cyclone will pass in an hour or so.
- ❑ Board up windows, tie down or lock up anything portable, and keep a supply of several days' drinking water.
- ❑ Outdoors, shelter in a cave or deep ditch, but not a vehicle; beware of high tides.

Earthquakes

- ❑ Keep away from sheets of glass; shelter on a ground floor in a corner or doorway.
- ❑ Outdoors, an open space is safest; lie flat, do not run.
- ❑ Avoid low ground and damaged buildings.

Dust storms

- ❑ Don't travel during a dust or sand storm; find shelter and cover your nose and mouth.

Thunder storms

- ❑ Avoid high ground, tall trees, metal equipment and moisture.
- ❑ Stay in a vehicle.

Snow

- ❑ Find or build makeshift shelter and sit out the blizzard.
- ❑ Cover your nose and mouth, lie flat and attempt to 'swim' to keep from sinking in an avalanche.
- ❑ Try to move upwards; kick a large hole before snow freezes.

7 NATURAL DISASTERS

Australia has its fair share of natural disasters. With luck you can avoid them, but if this is not possible, there are ways to increase your chances of survival. If you have time, think carefully before disaster strikes; plan how you can best survive the immediate crisis and the aftermath; prepare yourself, others and your surroundsings as best you can, and secure what you are likely to need.

Fires

It is better to avoid bushfires than to have to deal with them. To do so, remind yourself of the signs that a bushfire could be in the offing:

- ❑ drought or a prolonged stretch without rain which dries out bush and grasslands
- ❑ day(s) of extreme heat and low humidity
- ❑ strong winds
- ❑ smell or sight of smoke
- ❑ animals behaving unusually

If most of these signs are present, avoid planning or going into the bush or on long trips. If you live in an area that could be threatened by bushfires, keep the radio on and listen to all news bulletins. Do not light any fires (including cigarettes) outside on fire-danger days, and ensure that children cannot get at matches. If you hear that a bushfire is anywhere near your area, act immediately to secure the safety of yourself and your party, your pets, stock and other animals, and your property. (Securing houses and other property against bushfire is outside the scope of this book, but there are some excellent books on the subject.)

If you are unable to avoid bushfire, there are a number of important points to remember, firstly about the behaviour of fire. Fire travels faster up hill, so do not flee to higher ground – move downhill. Fire usually kills by radiant heat before either smoke or flame can harm a victim, and radiant heat travels in a straight line. Protect yourself by putting something solid between you and the oncoming fire – an earth wall or ditch, a car, a wall, even a pure woollen blanket (preferably wet) and sturdy boots can offer some protection. Fire can travel faster than you can run, especially up a hill, so don't try to outrun it unless you are very confident that you can easily and quickly reach safety. Similarly, don't run through a fire unless you can see that it is both low and narrow (no more than a metre or so in height and depth) and there is clear ground within easy reach. Don't run or drive into smoke if you can't see a safe haven within easy reach. The fire front, and the most intense heat, will pass within a few minutes – if you can survive that your chances of survival are good.

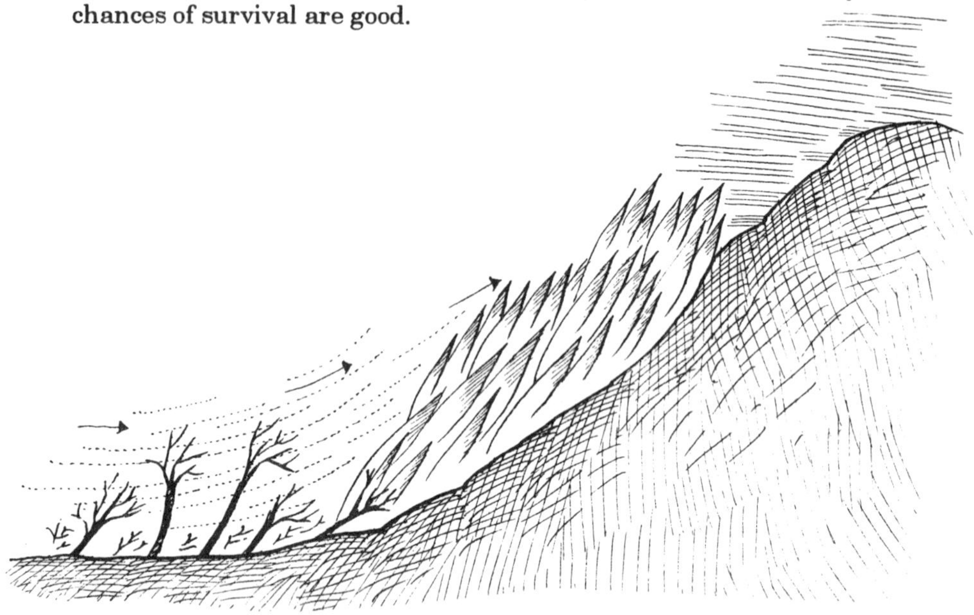

Fire travels faster up hill.

If you are caught in your vehicle by fire, your chances of survival are better if you stay in it than if you are outside it. Leave the lights on so the vehicle can be seen, but turn the engine off. Close all windows and air vents tightly and, as the fire approaches, get down below the level of the windows. If you have anything to cover the inside of the side windows (aluminium shades, rugs or towels) hang it up and wet it if possible. Sip water to prevent dehydration. The fuel tank is unlikely to explode, even if the fire is hot enough to shatter the windows. It may blow off the fuel cap and the escaping gas could catch fire, but this is still not a reason for leaving your vehicle. If you leave your vehicle, you will be exposed to potentially deadly radiant heat.

One protective strategy that may work if the fire is not too close and you are in great danger is to burn an area ahead of the fire in which you can shelter. Make sure you judge the direction of the wind accurately – it can be gusting from all directions in front of a bushfire. Try to burn as large an area as possible to give you plenty of space to shelter in. Light your fire in as long a line as you can, at least ten or twenty metres. It will burn away from you in the same direction as the oncoming fire, using up all the fuel on the ground. When the heat of your fire has passed, quickly move onto the burnt ground and try to protect yourself against the radiant heat of the oncoming bushfire. Even a woollen blanket will help.

In the worst circumstances, if you find yourself trapped by a fire with little protection, *do not panic*. You should have taken what time there is to look for a safe refuge. An old man survived a fierce fire by standing calmly on bare ground wrapped in a woollen blanket while his friends panicked and died. Panic will prevent you thinking clearly and will increase your exhaustion. If you run you will very quickly exhaust yourself and your supplies of oxygen. Assess your surroundings and possessions. If possible, cover yourself from head to toe with pure wool – any exposed skin is dangerous. If you can keep the wool wet then do so. If you have water with you, keep yourself wet as the fire approaches. If you are on a bulldozer or other earth-moving equipment, clear some ground or heap up a protective wall of earth or dig a trench (clear of vegetation). Alternatively, heap earth onto a blanket or coat and pull it over yourself as you shelter on any clear ground or in a clear depression or ditch. Keep your mouth and nose covered, preferably with a wet cloth, and try to take slow shallow breaths. If your clothes catch fire *do not run*. The wind you create will fan the flames. *Stop, drop and roll* till the flames are extinguished.

Do not shelter in above-ground tanks – people have died in them. Large in-ground pools, creeks and dams offer better protection.

Floods and flooded rivers

If you know an area will be threatened by floods or is already flooded, stay away unless you have a very good reason to be there. Otherwise, before travelling into the countryside, check weather maps and keep an eye on weather signs so you have ample warning of heavy rain. If you have a radio with you, listen for reports of heavy rain or flooding upstream from your position. Whenever there is danger of flooding, stay away from low-lying areas, and never camp in a dry creek bed, even in the desert.

Rivers can be dangerous to cross at any time; flooded rivers can be deadly. Currents are unpredictable and much stronger than usual;

there may be submerged snags, deep holes or other hazards; debris may be floating just below the surface; icy water can sap your strength in minutes; and panic-stricken animals may endanger anyone trying to cross flood waters.

Only enter flood waters if you absolutely must, and even then take time to study the crossing before you begin. Choose an area of shallow water (often where the river is widest) and watch how the surface of the water behaves – it can help you understand what lies beneath. Submerged branches can trap feet or make you lose your balance. Keep clear of any obstructions. Make sure the bank on the other side is low so you can get out easily. At a bend, the current will be strongest on the outer curve, but the water may be much deeper on the inner curve. Take a long sturdy stick with you for balance and to probe the bottom, even if the crossing site looks shallow.

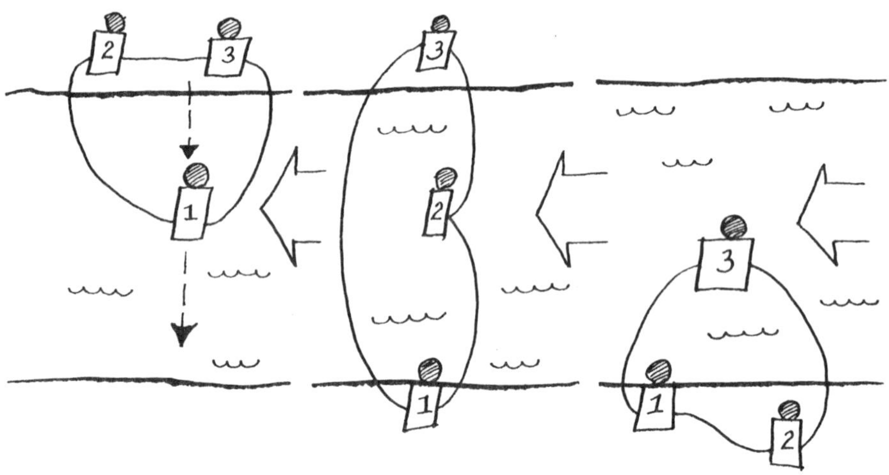

If you have a long rope and there are three or more of you, you can use an SAS technique. Tie the ends of the rope together securely to form a large loop. The strongest swimmer ties the rope around his or her chest and heads across the river while the other two hold the rope firmly on the bank; one at the point where the swimmer left, the second downstream. When the first person reaches the bank, the person downstream ties themselves to the rope and crosses, with the other two (one on each side of the river) holding the rope loop. Finally the third person crosses with the second person again taking up a position opposite and downstream from the place where the third person enters the water.

If you are swept away in flood waters do not waste your strength fighting the current. Try to grab something to help you keep afloat, and avoid dangling your legs in case they become entangled with snags. Try to make your way to shallow water where the current will be weaker, or to grab a tree and haul yourself out. Snakes may be sheltering in the tree, so be especially careful, and take a stick or break one off to protect yourself.

If you are caught in a flood, remember that drinking water can still be a problem – flood waters are probably polluted. Try to catch rain water, or if this is impossible, boil flood waters before drinking. After a flood, animal corpses can not only pollute waterways but spread disease, so be especially careful, and avoid any food or drink that has been touched by flood waters.

Cyclones and wind storms

Anyone who has seen photographs of the devastation caused by Cyclone Tracy will respect the power of cyclones. But even wind storms can be dangerous in certain circumstances. Cyclones are most likely to occur between November and April in the southern hemisphere (June to November in the northern hemisphere), but they can occur at any time. High winds rotate around the eye of the cyclone which is itself calm. If you are caught in a cyclone and a sudden calm falls, this is probably the eye of the cyclone passing over rather than the end of the wind. Stay where you are in case the winds return; the eye will usually pass in an hour or so and then the winds will blow just as fiercely but in the opposite direction. If you are sheltering outside, you will have to move to the other side of whatever is protecting you.

There are usually cyclone warnings up to a day ahead of the wind. The best policy is to get out of its path, but only evacuate if you have time to get safely away. It is dangerous to be caught in a vehicle during a cyclone.

If you are at home, board up all the windows or close cyclone shutters and tie down or lock up anything that could be caught up by the wind. Make sure shutters and roof are in good repair and there are no loose sheets of iron. Leave a window open on the sheltered side of the house so that air pressure remains the same inside and outside the house, then stay away from all windows. Even if the roof comes off the house, think carefully before you leave. If the house is still sturdy, you are probably safer inside than out. Shelter under a heavy table or bed.

You will be safer on high ground than on a river bank or by the coast. The more solid the building you are in the better, especially if it has a cellar or you can get under a stairway, but stay clear of fireplaces in case the chimney is blown over. Make sure you have a supply of clean drinking water – it may have to last you several days. Keep a radio (battery operated) on in case any warnings or instructions are broadcast. It may be safest to switch off the power, but this will depend on the sturdiness of the building in which you are sheltering.

If you are forced to shelter out of doors, try to find a cave, dug-out or deep ditch. If none of these is available, then a solid outcrop of rock or some other really solid shelter can protect you. Keep away from anything that could be blown over or uprooted. Even a sheet of corrugated iron can be deadly in a high wind.

Earthquakes

Strong earthquakes are relatively rare in Australia. There is unlikely to be much warning, unless you are alert to the changes in the behaviour of domestic or wild animals, who become restless and nervous. If by chance you do have warning, secure a supply of fresh water, some food, a first aid kit, fire extinguisher, torch, and any other emergency supplies you may need. Turn off all services to your house (gas, electricity, water) and make sure there are no heavy items on top of wardrobes, shelves or in the roof space. Keep your radio (battery operated) tuned to a local radio station for news reports and warnings.

If you are outside when an earthquake strikes, *do not run*. Lie flat and make sure others do the same. If possible, avoid tall buildings, trees, towers or poles, as well as tunnels or caves. An open space is safest, and the top of a hill is safer than the slopes. Beaches well away from cliffs are safe during an earthquake, but leave quickly afterwards and get to high ground in case of tidal waves.

If you are in a vehicle, stop quickly but safely and stay in the vehicle. Lie down below the windows so that you will have some protection if the vehicle is crushed. After the earthquake, check carefully for fallen power lines and make sure the road or bridges have not been damaged before you drive away.

Inside a building, find a haven well away from large sheets of glass (windows, mirrors, etc.). A sturdy doorway or the corner of a room, a strong table or desk may all offer some protection. A cellar or the ground floor is safer than upper storeys. Do not get into a lift, and think twice about a stairwell – it could be a hazard if people panic.

After a severe earthquake your first task will be to tend to the injured. Hazards will include pollution from corpses, escaped sewage, etc., so all drinking water should be filtered and boiled. Keep away from damaged buildings – it is safer to rig up a light shelter from debris. If there is any danger of a gas leak, do not light a match or cigarette lighter and be careful with sparks from tools. Be careful exploring buildings – heavy things could fall out of cupboards, there could be spilt chemicals or live wires, and the building itself could be unsafe.

Dust and sand storms

It can be dangerous trying to travel in dust storms, so stay put unless you have very good reasons for moving. If you are caught without shelter, try to find something to protect yourself from flying sand, even if you have to huddle behind a log or large rock or, at worst, sit with your back to the wind. Cover your mouth and nose with a cloth to make breathing easier.

If you are in a vehicle, try to park it in a sheltered place or at least park it with the engine facing away from the wind. Block the exhaust pipe (don't burn yourself) and, if you can, cover the air filter, carburettor and distributor. The petrol cap will probably be dustproof, but if you have any doubts, try to seal it too. Keep the doors and windows closed, except for one window on the leeward side which should be left open for ventilation. After the storm, remove the exhaust plug and engine coverings and carefully check the engine.

The risk of being smothered or covered over completely in a dust storm is remote, and if you can move around at all you will be safe. But do not try to drive or move far during a storm. Navigation will be difficult or impossible, visibility will be poor, and landmarks could change or be obscured.

Thunder storms

If you happen to be caught in a thunder storm, the greatest danger is from lightning strikes and the charge dispersing through the ground. Lightning is more likely to strike high points – rock outcrops, solitary trees, etc., so stay well away from these and from high ground. Anything metal will conduct electricity, so keep well away from any metal equipment, tent poles, pack frames, vehicles, etc, unless you can shelter inside a car. Even if the car is struck by lightning, you should be safe. You will be safest in a valley or on low-lying ground. If you cannot get away from high ground, sit on something that will insulate you, making sure your feet are off the ground and you are curled into a tight ball. A sleeping mat or coil of rope are suitable, but only if they are dry. If this is impossible, lie as flat as you can and stay there until the storm passes over.

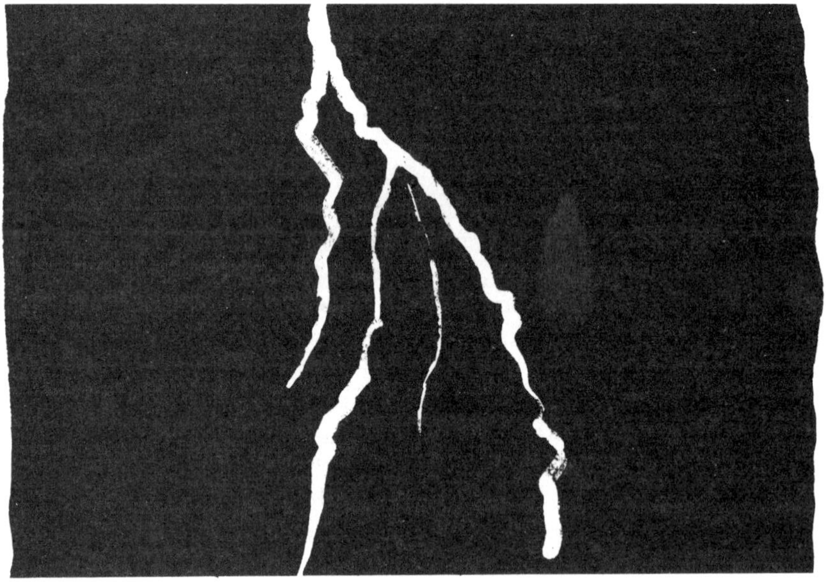

Snow

Blizzards and white-outs

In high country, snow can fall suddenly and unexpectedly, even in the middle of summer. If you are unprepared for travelling in snow and you have adequate shelter, it may be best to simply wait till the snow melts. In summer or late spring, snow falls will usually melt quickly. In a white-out, you may not be able to travel anyway – your depth perception will be unreliable, and if you are on skis you may not be able to judge the slope of terrain quickly enough to proceed safely. Unless you are very close to reliable shelter, it may be best to find makeshift shelter and sit out the blizzard, otherwise you could quickly exhaust yourself.

Avalanches

Avalanches are uncommon hazards in Australia, but less rare in countries with more extensive snowfields and heavier snowfalls. A few simple rules may help you survive. Cover your nose and mouth so you do not inhale snow – it can drown you almost as effectively as water. Throw away your pack or anything else that is likely to drag you down or make it difficult for you to move beneath the snow. Lie flat and attempt to 'swim' (freestyle) to keep towards the top of the fall. Once the avalanche stops, quickly kick as large a hole around yourself as you can before the snow freezes, trying to work your way towards the surface. Try to conserve as much energy as you can so you can shout to rescuers when they arrive.

SUMMARY

- ❑ Too much heat or cold can kill.
- ❑ Avoid sunburn with hat, clothing and sunscreen.
- ❑ Treat sunburn with cold water and a cool drink; do not burst blisters.
- ❑ Treat prickly heat by removing clothes, washing in cool water then replacing dry clothes.
- ❑ Treat heat cramps and heat exhaustion with rest in shade and a pinch of salt in drinking water.
- ❑ Treat heatstroke victim in the shade by wetting underclothes and fanning to cool.
- ❑ Wind and wetness increase chilling.
- ❑ Wear wool in cold conditions.
- ❑ Treat trench foot by drying and elevating feet while they gradually warm.
- ❑ Treat frostbite by heating gradually but not rubbing.
- ❑ Treat snow blindness with a blindfold in a darkened place.
- ❑ Treat hypothermia by preventing further heat loss then gradually warming. Give warm drinks and sugary food if conscious. Do not give alcohol or heat rapidly.

8 TEMPERATURE EXTREMES

Extremes of temperature can make an otherwise safe environment hazardous. Misreading a map on a bushwalk can sometimes be little more than a nuisance, but if the weather suddenly changes, bringing nothing more dramatic than rain, low temperatures and wind, you could soon be suffering from hypothermia unless you have the right clothing and equipment. Similarly, a fishing trip in an open boat can easily become hazardous if the engine fails and the sun beats down all day on people unprotected by either clothing, sunscreen or hats and without drinking water. Heatstroke can be life-threatening.

If you plan to spend time outdoors, make sure you familiarise yourself with the climate of the region into which you will be travelling and take clothing, footwear and equipment suitable for any weather you might encounter. Check weather maps for several days before your trip so you have an idea of what the weather might be and how it might change. An emergency 'space blanket' takes up little room and can be a life-saver if you are stranded.

Effects of heat

Heat can kill. In bushfires it is usually the radiant heat that kills a person before the flames or smoke have any effect. Similarly, exposure to the heat of the sun can make you ill and, eventually, kill you.

The human body is affected not only by heat outside itself but also by heat generated within from exercise, and it has a number of ways of cooling itself, or more properly, losing heat.

Sweating

When the body sweats, salty fluid is produced by sweat glands in the skin. As the sweat evaporates it carries heat away from the body, thereby cooling it. The effectiveness of sweating depends on humidity and air movement: in hot, dry, windy conditions sweat will cool the body more effectively; in hot, still, humid conditions it will be less effective.

In a hot humid climate, heat does not have to be severe to be dangerous. In such conditions even a little exercise can overheat the body to such an extent that it is unable to cool itself. The body's temperature rises and, should it go higher than 41°C, sudden collapse, unconsciousness and even death may follow.

With heavy sweating, many litres of water are lost each day as well as many grams of salt. Lack of salt causes heat cramps, and loss of water may result in thicker blood that cannot circulate properly. Dehydration also harms many other systems within the body.

Dilation of blood vessels

If a person becomes overheated, the small blood vessels close to the surface of the skin expand to allow more blood through. Heat is lost from this blood into the environment, thus cooling the body. This is why a hot person looks flushed and feels hot to the touch.

Eating

A person's metabolic rate is lower in hot weather and their need for food is thus reduced. Less food produces less heat causing the body fewer cooling problems. If you don't feel like eating much in hot weather, listen to your body and don't eat.

Hair erector muscles

In hot weather the tiny muscles that can make your hair 'stand on end' relax so that the hairs lie flat to the skin and are less likely to trap heat. The opposite to this is goosebumps in cold weather.

Overheating

Overheating can cause minor discomfort at least, death at most. Some of the conditions are listed below. Their treatment is covered in the section on first aid.

Sunburn

Sunburn is never pleasant, but if your survival is at stake, sunburn could affect your chances. If your skin is exposed it will be absorbing the maximum amount of heat from the sun, adding to your body heat. Once the skin is burned it may blister, losing precious fluid that you may not be able to replace. The pain of sunburn may prevent you sleeping, prevent you moving freely and lower your spirits, the cumulative effect of which could be dangerous to a person already weak. Lastly, you will have exposed yourself to the risk of skin cancer. Even if you survive your current ordeal, it may still, in time, kill you.

Sunburn can be especially severe on ice or snow, on water or in the desert. Rays can be reflected up into the face even though a person is wearing a hat.

The best treatment for sunburn is avoidance. Make sure as much exposed skin as possible is kept covered by light clothing. Wear a hat. If you have any sun screen, use it on exposed skin.

Prickly heat

This skin irritation is caused by excessive sweating combined with friction from clothing which block sweat glands. Drinking extra water may only exacerbate the problem.

Muscle cramps

These cramps result from salt loss due to excessive sweating. They may be accompanied by dizziness, shallow breathing or even vomiting. These should be taken seriously or heat exhaustion may follow.

Heat exhaustion

If you or someone in your party looks pale, has cold or clammy skin and feels weak or dizzy, faints or perhaps suffers from cramps, and has a weak or rapid pulse, then they have heat exhaustion. This can be caused by heat and humidity alone, without exposure to the sun.

Heatstroke

This is the most dangerous condition caused by heat. The skin appears flushed and dry and feels hot. Sweating stops, the person's temperature rises and their pulse becomes strong and rapid. They may suffer from a severe headache and vomit, finally becoming unconscious.

Effects of cold

Cold can kill quietly and insidiously. A walk that would be easy and safe in fine weather can become life-threatening in wet, cold and windy conditions; a person can be dead from cold in as little as five hours.

The body has mechanisms for maintaining a constant temperature so long as the environmental temperature is not too extreme. It has a number of ways of heating itself and retaining heat.

Shivering

Any exercise warms the body because it increases heat production in the muscles. But even if you don't exercise in cold weather, your body will do it for you – it shivers. Like any exercise, shivering uses energy, and energy is needed by the body for heat. Without extra food, shivering can use up the body's energy reserves and add to the danger.

Eating

In cold weather the body's metabolism speeds up, increasing a person's appetite for food. Extra food increases the amount of heat the body produces and helps to maintain its temperature.

Hair erector muscles

These muscles contract in cold weather and body hair stands on end. This helps protect the surface of the body from cold winds and maintains a layer of still air around the body which is slowly warmed and helps reduce further heat loss. In animals and birds you will notice that their fur, hair or feathers fluff out in cold weather due to these muscles.

Sweating

In cold weather sweat glands stop working, thus reducing heat loss through evaporation.

Constriction of blood vessels

In cold weather blood vessels near the surface of the skin constrict to reduce the blood flow and prevent too much heat escaping into the environment. As a result the skin looks pale and feels cold to the touch. Note that this does not apply to babies, who are unable to regulate their temperatures. A baby can freeze to death while still looking pink and healthy.

Chilling and freezing

Cold can give you no more than chilblains or it can kill. If you are cold and wet, wind can reduce your temperature even further. For example, at around -25°C exposed flesh may begin to freeze. If there is a 20 to 30 knot wind, the temperature need only be -12°C to freeze your flesh. In other words, wind can double the effects of cold.

Water will carry heat from the body far more efficiently than air, so even a minor wetting can seriously affect your body's chances of dealing with cold. Woollen clothing is less likely to absorb moisture and retains more body heat when it is wet than other materials, so consider it when you may be confronted with cold or damp conditions. A hat is essential – up to one-third of body heat can be lost through the head. In extremely cold conditions, make sure you expose as little skin as possible. Clothing should have drawstrings at all openings or be fastened with string or ties to prevent warm air escaping.

If you fall into icy water you will have to act quickly. Get out immediately before you lose consciousness. Rolling in snow will absorb some of the wetness, but you will then have to get to shelter immediately and change into dry clothes.

In water colder than 2°C a person can die in less than 45 minutes. In water colder than 10°C it may take up to three hours to die, and if the water is below 20°C a person may last no longer than 12 hours. Above this critical temperature (20°C) a person may survive indefinitely if they do not become exhausted.

If you have a life jacket and find yourself floating in cold water, you can reduce the rate at which your body loses heat by pressing your arms to your sides, bringing your legs up to protect your groin, and keeping as still as possible. If there are several of you, huddle together with the sides of your chests pressed together to reduce heat loss.

If there are babies, children or elderly people in your group, they will be at far greater risk of hypothermia than adults. This also applies to the injured or sick.

Trench foot

If for some reason your feet are wet and cold for long periods you may suffer from trench foot, with pins and needles, numbness and occasional shooting pains. Your feet may turn purple, swell and become blistered.

To avoid trench foot, wear sturdy waterproof shoes or boots with two or more pairs of socks for warmth.

Frostbite

Frostbite is the result of skin freezing, usually on the extremities. The patches may prick at first before becoming numb and waxy, mottled blue or grey-white. Eventually they become hard, swollen and painful, finally blistering or ulcerating, turning red or gangrenous, and lastly dropping off.

Avoidance is the best policy with frostbite. Wear enough clothing to keep warm; keep dry; never touch metal with your bare skin or allow skin to come into contact with petrol. Keep blood circulating by moving the muscles in the face, hands and feet. At the first sign of waxy skin, begin treatment.

Snow blindness

If the eyes are exposed to too much glare, whether or not the day is clear or overcast, they can be temporarily blinded. At first they are merely sensitive to the glare, then the person will begin to squint or blink and complain that their eyes feel gritty. Everything will take on a pinkish tinge.

To avoid snow blindness, rub charcoal underneath the eyes to reduce glare and protect your eyes with dark glasses, goggles, or at worst a length of cloth or bark with slits cut in it.

Hypothermia

A person does not have to be caught in a blizzard to suffer hypothermia, especially if they are old or frail or very young. Prolonged exposure to cold, even if the temperature is above freezing, can lead to hypothermia, especially if certain conditions exist that exacerbate the effects of cold. These include exhaustion, the taking of alcohol or certain drugs, wet or damp clothes, exposure to wind, illness or injury, infancy or old age.

If you suspect you or anyone in your party may be starting to suffer from hypothermia, do not try to keep going but stop and begin treatment if you can find any sort of shelter. At least eat some food and rest out of the wind (see the section on first aid for treatment).

Hypothermia begins to develop when the body temperature falls below 35°C and is irreversible once it passes 25°C. Do not rely on a normal thermometer to test a person's temperature at these levels – assume they are at risk and treat them accordingly.

At first the person may only complain of feeling cold. Their skin becomes pale and cold, although babies may retain their pink colouring and still be at risk because of their inability to control their temperature. They will begin to shiver uncontrollably, but then the shivering fades away and they become uncoordinated and speak with a slur. Next they become irrational and uncomprehending, with sudden bursts of energy interrupting a general lethargy or stupor. They may complain of headaches, blurred vision or stomach pain. Their pulse and breathing slow and they eventually lose consciousness. Finally their heartbeat and breathing become almost impossible to detect and if they are not treated they will die. Even when no pulse or heartbeat can be detected, a person should be treated and not assumed to be dead.

The effects of low temperatures on a person can be exacerbated by exhaustion, lack of food, anxiety, injuries that prevent free movement, poor clothing or shelter, and immersion in cold water. Some of these conditions may be unavoidable, but with adequate knowledge and planning, many of them can be avoided.

Babies and infants can suffer hypothermia while still appearing to be a healthy pink colour. Watch for symptoms such as drowsiness and limpness, refusal to eat, unusual quietness. In the elderly, hypothermia can often be mistaken for illness such as a stroke or heart attack. Even if the temperature is not extreme, consider the effects of inadequate food, heating and exercise.

SUMMARY

Following each dangerous creature is the main risk from it, plus treatment. For PIM (Pressure/Immobilisation Method), see below as well as section on first aid.

- ❑ *Ants, bees and wasps*: allergic response; (remove bee sting); ice water or PIM and resuscitation for allergic response.
- ❑ *Blue-ringed octopus*: death; PIM, resuscitation, medical attention.
- ❑ *Box jellyfish and certain other jellyfish*: pain, death; vinegar on tentacles before removing them, resuscitation, medical attention.
- ❑ *Cone shells*: death; PIM, resuscitation, medical attention.
- ❑ *Crocodile*: injury, death; apply pressure to stem bleeding, medical attention.
- ❑ *Funnelwebs and similar spiders (not redbacks)*: death; PIM, medical attention.
- ❑ *Platypus*: pain; medical attention.
- ❑ *Redback spiders*: pain, death; no PIM; medical attention.
- ❑ *Shark*: injury, death; apply pressure to stem bleeding, medical attention.
- ❑ *Snakes, land and sea*: death; PIM, medical attention.
- ❑ *Stinging fish*: pain, serious illness, possibly death; hot water on wound, medical attention.
- ❑ *Ticks*: illness, death; remove entire tick without squeezing; PIM, medical attention.

PIM (Pressure/Immobilisation Method)

- ❑ Keep person still. Apply broad pressure bandage firmly over the bite and extend down to the end of the limb and up the limb towards the heart as far as possible. Apply a splint. Bind splint firmly to leg or put splinted arm in a sling. Get to hospital as soon as possible. The bandage should not be removed until the doctor has the appropriate drugs and treatment ready. Do not cut the wound or the limb, or apply a tourniquet.

9 DANGEROUS CREATURES

There are many creatures in Australia and its waters that can kill or injure people; the best policy is to avoid them. If this is impossible, and you or someone in your party is bitten or stung, the pressure/immobilisation method of first aid, described above and in more detail in the section on first aid, is usually the best treatment. But there are some exceptions.

Exceptions to PIM treatment

Ants

Remove the ant(s). Use iced water on the sting unless there is a severe allergic response. In that case the pressure/immobilisation method will stop the venom spreading while you get to a doctor. Resuscitation may be necessary in very severe responses.

Bees

Carefully remove the sting, being careful not to squeeze the poison sack at the end of it, then use iced water unless there is a severe allergic response. In that case the pressure/immobilisation method will stop the venom spreading while you get to a doctor. Resuscitation may be necessary in very severe responses.

Box jellyfish

Pour vinegar over the tentacles before you try to remove them. After five minutes they will be inactive and can be wiped off. Get to a doctor immediately and begin resuscitation if breathing starts to fail.

Jellyfish

Pour vinegar over the tentacles before you try to remove them. After five minutes they will be inactive and can be wiped off. Get to a doctor quickly if there is a severe reaction.

Redback spiders

Catch the spider for identification. Do not restrict the movement of the venom, which is very slow. Get to a doctor quickly.

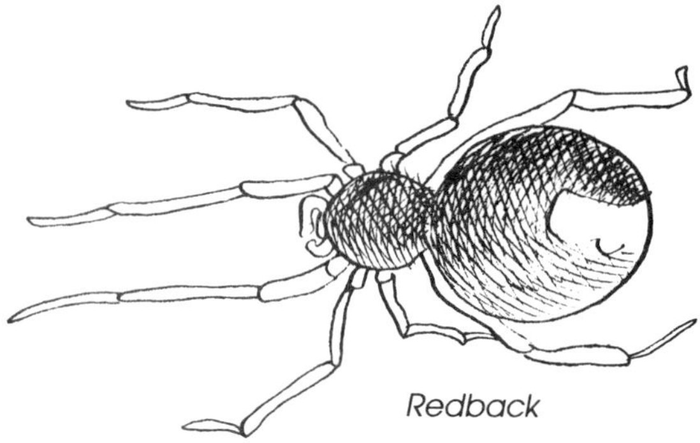

Redback

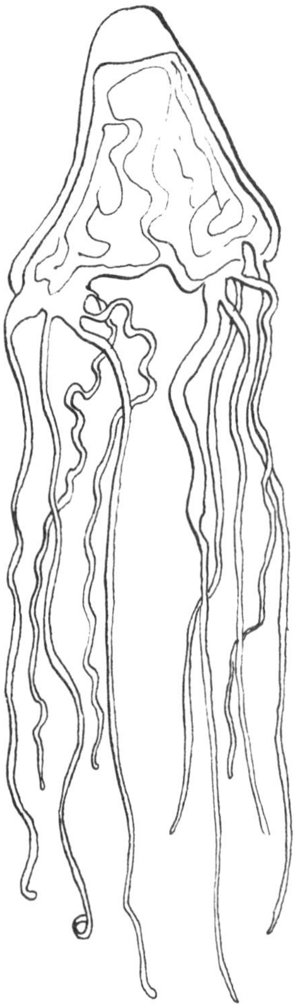

Box jellyfish

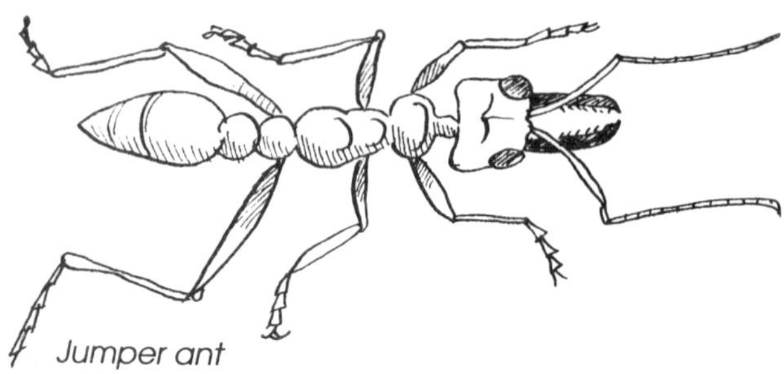

Jumper ant

Tick

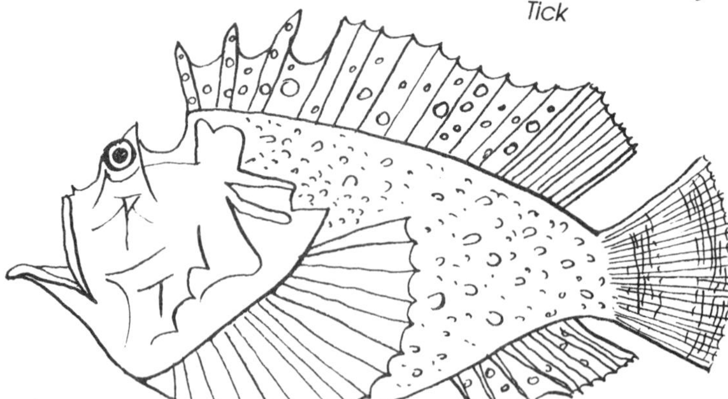

Stonefish

Stonefish and other stinging fish

Pain relief is important. If you cannot reach a doctor quickly, apply water hot enough to bear, but not scalding, to the wound; this may deactivate and disperse some of the venom, thus reducing the severity of the pain. If there is a severe reaction resuscitation may be necessary.

Ticks

Australian paralysis ticks should be removed immediately. The whole body and mouth parts must be extracted. If the tick has only been burrowing for a few hours it can be wiped off. If it has burrowed in it may have to be removed with sharp tweezers or the points of a pair of scissors. *Do not try to squeeze it out* – more poison will enter the victim. A poison such as chloroform, ether, or turpentine that can safely be applied to the skin may help to dislodge the tick. Once it has been removed, the pressure/immobilisation method can be used.

Wasps

Wasps can sting repeatedly. Remove the wasp(s) and use iced water unless there is a severe allergic response. In that case the pressure/immobilisation method will stop the venom spreading while you get to a doctor. Resuscitation may be necessary in very severe responses.

Snakes

Identification

No Australian lizards are poisonous, and not every Australian snake is either, but those that are venomous are the most poisonous in the world. Even experts have trouble distinguishing between some snakes, so a knowledge of where certain snakes occur is often useful.

Tasmania

copperhead; black tiger snake.

Victoria

mainland tiger snake; common or eastern brown snake; gwadar or western brown snake (north); copperhead; red-bellied black snake; small-scaled or fierce snake (possibly in extreme north-west corner); eastern small-eyed snake (east).

New South Wales and the Australian Capital Territory

mainland tiger snake; common or eastern brown snake; gwadar or western brown snake; copperhead (east); red-bellied black snake;

mulga or king brown snake; blue-bellied or spotted black snake (north); death adder; taipan (north-east); small-scaled or fierce snake (near border of SA and Qld); rough-scaled or Clarence River snake (far east); eastern small-eyed snake (east); broad-headed snake (east); Stephen's banded snake (east); pale-headed snake (east).

Queensland

mainland tiger snake (south); common or eastern brown snake; gwadar or western brown snake; speckled brown snake; red-bellied black snake (east); mulga or king brown snake; blue-bellied or spotted black snake (south); Collett's snake; death adder; taipan (north and east); small-scaled or fierce snake (near border of NT, SA, and NSW); rough-scaled or Clarence River snake (far east); eastern small-eyed snake (east); Stephen's banded snake (east); pale-headed snake (east).

Northern Territory

common or eastern brown snake; gwadar or western brown snake; speckled brown snake; mulga or king brown snake; death adder; taipan (north); small-scaled or fierce snake (near border of Qld and SA).

Western Australia

black tiger snake; common or eastern brown snake (north); gwadar or western brown snake; dugite; mulga or king brown snake; death adder; taipan (north).

South Australia

common or eastern brown snake (south); gwadar or western brown snake; red-bellied black snake (south-east); mulga or king brown snake; death adder; small-scaled or fierce snake (near border of NT, Qld, and NSW).

Avoiding snakes

The best policy is to leave snakes well alone. Generally they will not attack unless they are frightened or you have cut off their means of escape. Like other native Australian animals, snakes are protected, but if someone has been bitten, it is useful to take the (dead!) snake to hospital with the victim for identification. Only attempt to kill the snake if it is completely safe to do so and you can kill it quickly without compromising the care of the person who has been bitten. Without the corpse, it is often difficult to identify a snake, but avoid heroics.

The best treatment for snake bite is to avoid being bitten in the first place. Check before stepping over a log or other obstacle that obscures

your view of the ground, especially when walking into the sun. A snake may be basking in the warmth on the far side of the log. When a snake may be nearby, many bushwalkers believe that stamping or walking heavily will drive it away. Because snakes are deaf, these vibrations may well be a good method of communicating your presence. If you are going to rummage around in hollow logs, rabbit or animal burrows, or long grass, look before you do so, and consider wearing thick gloves. Sturdy shoes and loose strong clothing are the best protection in snake country, and no-one should wander through long grass or beside creeks or swamps with bare legs and sandals. In some parts of Australia, snakes are active on warm nights, so use a strong torch if you are walking at night, even a few steps to go to the toilet.

Snakebite

If you suspect that you or someone in your party has been bitten, start first aid measures at once – it is not worth waiting until symptoms appear! Snake fangs are very sharp and thin, so a bite may not be obvious.

Snake venom contains poisons that act on nerves, causing paralysis. It may also contain substances that prevent blood clotting and damage blood cells or muscles. Symptoms may appear within a quarter of an hour or after several hours, and may include paralysis of facial muscles followed by paralysis of the chest and diaphragm; sweating; nausea, vomiting or diarrhoea; faintness or drowsiness; blurred vision or headache; unconsciousness.

First-aid for snake bite (PIM) is repeated in the Summary in an abbreviated form, but see the section on first aid for details; old methods such as cutting the wound, applying tourniquets, etc., usually do more harm to the victim than good.

Insects, spiders and scorpions

Ants

Australia has a number of stinging ants, some of which can be dangerous to humans who develop an allergy to the venom. The most common dangerous ants are bull ants, jumping ants and green-headed ants; the latter are tropical or sub-tropical, the former are found in more temperate areas.

An ant sting is immediately painful, and multiple stings, especially on a child, can cause severe pain and shock. The greatest danger, though, is an acquired allergy after more than one bite. This can result in a rash, swelling, breathing difficulties or even collapse. Antihistamines are said to be helpful if the victim is conscious, but the best policy is to get medical assistance promptly.

Bees

People can develop an allergy to bee stings in much the same way as they do to ants, with similarly serious results. If an allergy is suspected, get medical assistance for the victim as quickly as possible. Otherwise scrape the sting out of the wound to avoid squeezing more venom out of the gland (the barbed sting will have pulled away from the bee's abdomen with the venom gland, fatally injuring the bee). Take special care to avoid stings to the throat or mouth because these could swell and obstruct the airways.

Centipedes

Centipedes can be found throughout Australia. Their fangs can give people a painful bite and inject venom, although to date nobody in Australia has died as a result. Generally no first aid is required unless the victim becomes ill or pain persists.

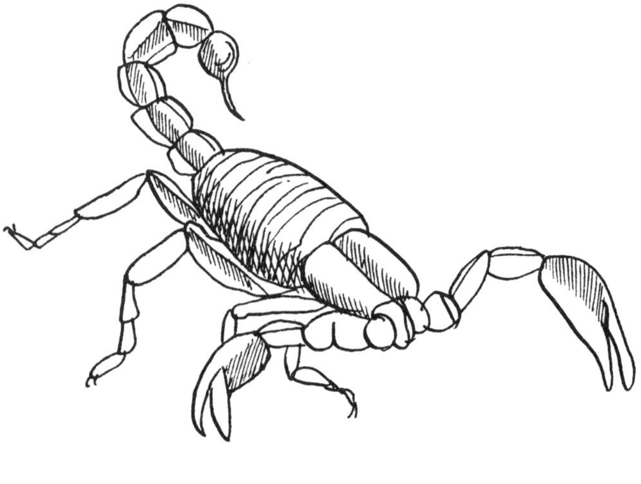

Scorpions

In Australia, scorpions are widespread but fortunately not lethal to adults, although a sting could kill a baby. In the tropics they are larger and more dangerous than their southerly relatives and their stings can produce severe pain and swelling. The stings of smaller scorpions are less severe. The sting is located in the tail, which the creature will raise threateningly if alarmed.

Spiders

Unfortunately Australia has some of the most dangerous spiders in the world, but little is known about most Australian spiders because victims can rarely identify the spider that bit them. If you are bitten by a spider, try to catch it and take it with you when you seek treatment.

Black house-spiders

These common spiders are found throughout Australia and can be recognised by their untidy funnel-shaped webs. They rarely grow beyond 1.5 cm and are grey or faded rusty black. Their bites can be very painful and occasionally cause sweating, weakness and vomiting. There is no particular first aid, but if the victim becomes ill, get them to a doctor quickly, taking the spider with you.

Fiddleback spiders

The overseas relatives of these spiders have caused serious illness and death to their victims, but so far no fatalities have been attributed to the Australian fiddleback. These small brown spiders are found around Adelaide and in other parts of South Australia. There is no particular first aid, but if the victim becomes ill, get them to a doctor quickly, taking the spider with you.

Funnelwebs

Funnelweb spiders are found in Victoria, South Australia and Tasmania, but the Sydney, Northern or Tree-dwelling varieties, amongst the most dangerous spiders in the world, are the ones that cause most concern. They are particularly aggressive, with fangs strong enough to pierce a child's fingernail.

The venom of the male Sydney funnelweb is five times more poisonous than that of the female, but even this is surpassed by the venom of the female northern or tree-dwelling funnelweb. Bites from the Sydney female funnelweb usually cause little more than pain at the site of the bite; those from the male cause muscle twitching, excessive sweating and production of large amounts of saliva and tears. The toxin also affects blood vessels in such a way that shock and brain damage can result. An antivenom is available, and victims should be taken to hospital immediately. This spider is found within an area roughly 200 km from Sydney.

Webs of funnelwebs are usually white and can be tubular rather than funnel shaped; males often roam far from webs, so don't rely on the presence of a web for identification.

The northern or tree-dwelling funnelweb, as the name suggests, lives in thick forest on the east coast of Australia in New South Wales and southern Queensland. They are not always above ground, and can be found in tunnels or fallen logs. The female is huge, and her bite can cause intense pain, vomiting and sweating, delirium and coma. The antivenom of the Sydney funnelweb is effective against this spider too.

Mouse spiders

These aggressive spiders are a type of trapdoor spider and are widespread throughout Australia. The male has a distinctive red head and fangs, but the more dangerous female is a plain black heavy spider. Her venom is extremely poisonous. Burrows run vertically into the ground and are lined with silk and sealed with two oval doors. There is no particular first aid, but if the victim becomes ill, get them to a doctor quickly, taking the spider with you.

Redbacks

Redbacks are common throughout Australia and have even entered our folklore. The much smaller male is not considered dangerous, but the female bears a warning stripe of bright red on her abdomen, although this can sometimes be paler or even grey. These small elegant black spiders are not aggressive, and keep to themselves in fine untidy webs in dark out-of-the-way places. The effects of a bite are distinctive: after the initial sting, the pain intensifies and spreads to other areas. The bitten limb sweats, even though the rest of the body may remain dry. The poison moves slowly, and no attempt should be made to impede its progress with a bandage or tourniquet. Get medical help as soon as is practicable, but don't panic. There is usually plenty of time to administer antivenom.

Wolf spiders

There are many species of wolf spiders found throughout Australia, most of them marked with grey and black or brown and black patterns.

Few grow beyond medium size, and most would be encountered in gardens. After suspected or confirmed bites from wolf spiders, victims have suffered skin damage and even gangrene, as well as dangerous swellings and even kidney damage. There is no particular first aid, but if the victim becomes ill, get them to a doctor quickly, taking the spider with you.

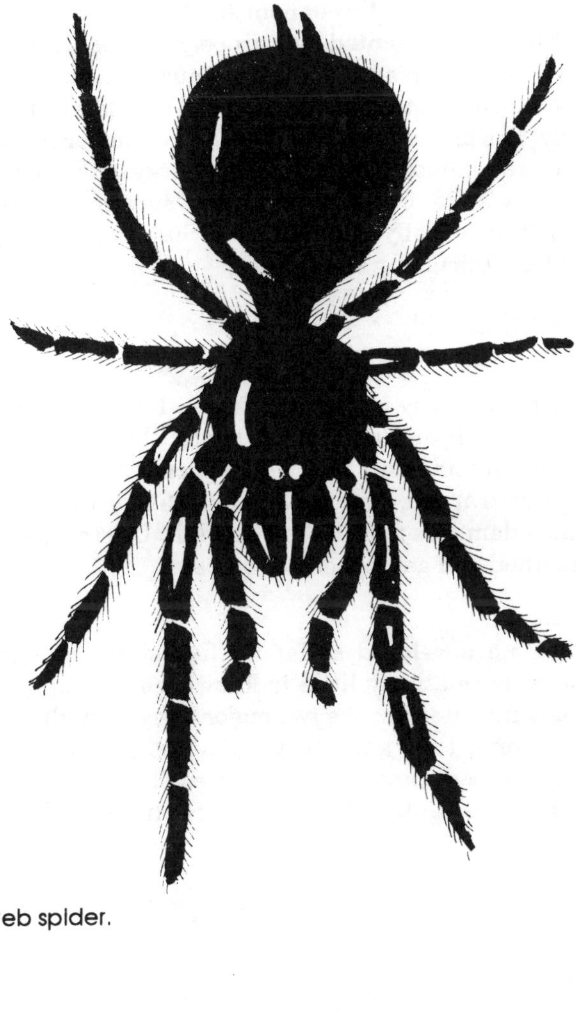

Funnelweb spider.

Ticks

Australian paralysis ticks infest country along the eastern edge of the continent. The poisonous saliva of ticks can cause serious allergies in certain people as well as paralysis that can sometimes be fatal. Animals can also be at risk. After a trip into tick country, check everyone (including the pet dog) for signs of ticks – they can hide in skin creases and amongst hair, so be thorough. Check daily for six days. There is a tick antitoxin available. First aid is described above.

Wasps

Native wasps are widespread throughout Australia and their numbers have recently been supplemented by European wasps. There is also a large wingless wasp known as a blue ant because of its iridescent blue body. Unlike bees, wasps' stings are not barbed and, like ants, they can sting repeatedly. The pain and shock of sufficient numbers of stings can be fatal, but a more common danger is from allergy to the venom. Take care when drinking sweet drinks from cans in summer – a swallowed wasp could inflict potentially fatal stings to the throat or tongue, the resultant swelling obstructing the airways.

Sea creatures

Sea snakes

Sea snakes are particularly common in tropical waters, but they are also found as far south as Tasmania. Usually they will not harm a person unless they are handled. This can happen inadvertently if a sea snake is netted or trapped, and is especially likely when fishing at night. The venom damages muscles and can kill. Use the pressure/immobilisation method and get to a doctor quickly.

Poisonous fish

The only antivenom developed so far for fish stings is against the stonefish, otherwise relatively little is known about Australian fish venoms. Pain and infection are the two major dangers with fish stings. If pain is very severe, the victim may go into shock, so get medical attention quickly in these cases. Wounds can easily become infected, so a tetanus shot is also essential. The following fish can be dangerous.

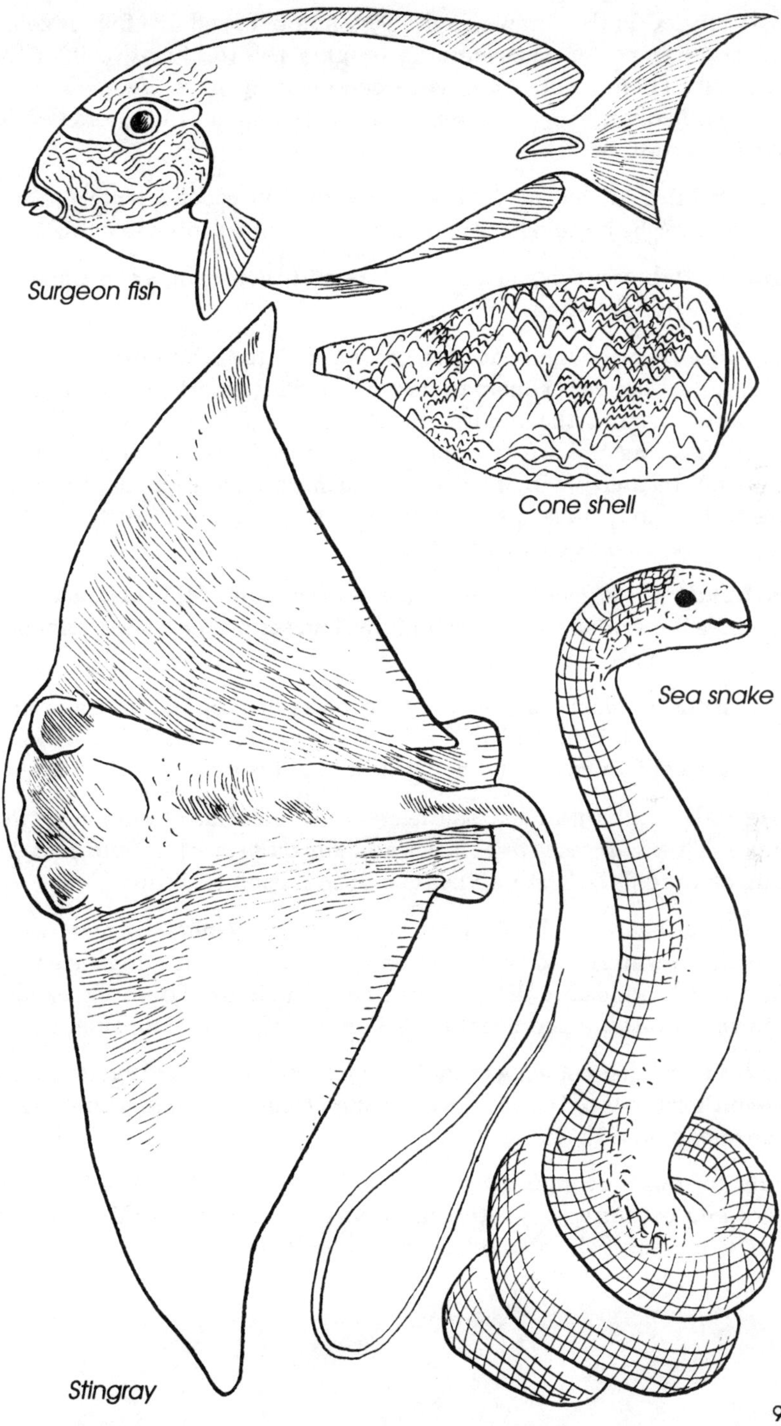
Surgeon fish
Cone shell
Sea snake
Stingray

Butterfly cod (also known as fire cod, lion fish, red-fire fish or zebra fish) occur in waters surrounding roughly the top two-thirds of the continent. Their spines can cause excruciating pain. People can be stung while diving, or while handling fish in an aquarium, and deaths have been reported.

Catfish (also known as cobblers) occur in all coastal waters. They should never be handled or their spines will inflict intense pain.

Cobbler fish occur in southern waters and their spines can cause an extremely painful sting.

Cone shells, although beautiful, contain fish that can inflict a deadly sting. A dart delivers venom to the victim, who experiences pain, then numbness around the mouth. Paralysis can follow, then difficulty breathing, coma and death. Apply the pressure/immobilisation method immediately and begin mouth to mouth resuscitation if breathing falters. This may have to be continued for a long time. Get the victim to a hospital as quickly as possible.

Flatheads: the spines on the head and underside of this delicious fish can cause fishermen painful wounds, but no serious or lasting damage. They occur in all coastal waters.

Fortesque (or waspfish) occur in estuaries in eastern Australia and their spines can inflict painful stings. Skindivers and fishermen are most at risk of touching and being stung by this fish.

Frog fish occur in all but southern waters and are common in the tropics. They can survive out of water for quite a while and may be found on mud flats. Their spines can inflict a painful sting.

Ghouls (or bearded ghouls, Chinese ghouls or demon stingers) occur in northern waters and appear to be aggressive. Their stings are very painful and can lead to illness, swelling of the injured limb, shock and impaired breathing and heart beat. Pain relief is most important.

Goblin fish, also known as saddleheads, occur in waters surrounding the southern half of the continent. Stings from their spines can cause intense pain and shock.

Kroki (or bullrout, rock cod, scorpion fish or wasp fish) are found in rivers and estuaries of eastern and northern Australia. Most stings occur when the fish is trodden on or handled. Pain from even light contact with the spines is intense and can spread. Headache and vomiting may also occur.

Old wife, also known as the zebra fish, occurs in all Australian coastal waters and can inflict a painful sting if handled. Pain may be severe, and vomiting and headache sometimes occur.

Port Jackson shark, despite its name, occurs in waters surrounding the southern half of the continent. The spines on its back fins can cause a painful injury leading to weakness, and susceptible to infection. Fishermen and skindivers are most at risk.

Rabbit fish (also known as black spine fish, mimi, stinging bream or black trevally), occur in most Australian waters, but most commonly in northern Queensland. Their spines can produce painful stings.

Rat fish occur in deep waters surrounding the southern half of the continent. Their spine can cause tissue damage as well as poisoning, and they have dangerous teeth.

Scorpion fish are variously known as chained scorpion fish, cardinal scorpion fish, red scorpion cod and red rock cod. They occur in waters surrounding the eastern half of the continent and often injure fishermen who handle them carelessly. Pain and occasionally vomiting and collapse can result. See also Cobbler fish and Kroki.

Stingrays of various types are commonly found in Australian waters. Their tails contain a large spine which they can drive into their victims with great force if they are trodden on or approached too closely. If the wound is in a vulnerable organ, death can occur, but more commonly the legs are injured. Complications include tetanus and infection from debris left in the wound.

Stonefish are found in waters surrounding the top half of the continent. Their spines are strong enough to go through rubber soles and the venom causes extreme pain; if untreated, the poison can damage heart muscles. Most wounds result from people standing on the fish or handling it when out fishing.

Surgeon fish (or doctor fish, spinetail or tang) occur in all waters surrounding the top half or so of the continent. Fishermen who handle the fish after it has been caught can be injured, but it also attacks swimmers, presumably when it feels threatened. It can inflict deep cuts with great speed. Pain and bleeding are the main problems. Remove the victim from the water and apply pressure to stop bleeding.

Jellyfish

Queensland and northern Australian waters contain the two most dangerous jellyfish – the box jellyfish or sea wasp, and *Chiropsalmus* – as well as the irukandji, but all Australian coastal waters contain dangerous and potentially deadly jellyfish such as the blue bottle or Portuguese man-of-war, the jimble, stingers such as the mauve stinger or hairy stinger, mauve blubbers or sea blubbers.

Not only the tentacles but also the bell of some of these jellyfish can cause injury, and nobody should go near or touch a jellyfish if they can possibly avoid it. In the tropics, swim only at patrolled beaches and only when local people say it is safe to do so. The two most dangerous jellyfish are common in summer months in the north, but stings have occurred at other times of the year. Where tentacles stick to the skin, they should not be touched until they are first neutralised with vinegar, or they will fire off more poison capsules. An antivenom for box jellyfish is available, and victims should be taken to hospital immediately; resuscitation may be necessary on the way.

Blue-ringed octopus

These small octopus with their bright blue warning rings are unlikely to harm humans unless they are picked up or otherwise disturbed, whereupon they may inflict a potentially lethal bite with their parrot beaks. The injury may not be especially painful, but soon the tongue and lips will begin to tingle, sight and speech will become difficult, vomiting and collapse may follow within as little as ten minutes followed by paralysis which eventually prevents breathing and, without mouth-to-mouth resuscitation, causes death.

Use the pressure/immobilisation method immediately and resuscitation for as long as necessary. Get the victim to hospital as quickly as possible.

Salt water crocodiles

Since crocodiles were protected, their numbers have increased, and as recent news bulletins confirm, so has their threat to people. Fresh water crocodiles are relatively harmless, and can be identified by their long narrow snouts. The larger, heavier, blunter salt water crocodiles can easily kill. They are found in waterways throughout the top part of the continent, and despite their name, are equally at home in fresh or brackish water. During the wet season, vast areas of country can be flooded, allowing crocodiles to penetrate far inland and take up residence in apparently innocuous waterholes.

When travelling in the north, always observe crocodile warning signs, and never swim in a waterway unless you are positive it could not have been inundated during the wet. Upstream from a waterfall is often reasonably safe, but it is best to always ask the locals. Swimming in the sea can also be hazardous, and it is wise to get local advice before taking a dip.

Crocodiles can also attack on land, moving surprisingly quickly. Do not approach crocodile nests or baby crocodiles, and do not allow children to wander near waterways. Be alert yourself when you are near water, and avoid cleaning fish in or near the water.

Sharks

Australian waters contain a number of potentially dangerous sharks, such as white pointers, whalers, the grey nurse, tiger shark, reef sharks and makos. The Port Jackson shark poses a threat with its poisonous spines, located at the front of the two fins on its back, but the teeth and jaws of other sharks pose a more obvious and immediate threat.

To reduce the chance of a shark attack, never swim if you have a wound or are likely to leak blood into the water. Do not urinate, defecate or vomit in the water, or swim with or near a dog, or where berley has been thrown into the water, or with fish that have been speared or caught. Avoid schools of fish, too. Any of these could attract sharks.

Sharks will often circle their victims before attacking, sometimes even brushing against them. If this happens to you, try hard not to panic. If you thrash around in the water you are going to look more like a wounded fish to the shark and are more likely to provoke an attack; try to swim towards safety with strong even strokes.

If there are a number of you in the water, group together and face the shark. Finally, if the shark seems ready to attack, try any of the following before you are tempted to strike out or kick the shark – its rough hide will abrade your skin and may make you even more tempting: feint at the shark to try to discourage it, shouting underwater or slapping the surface; keep facing the shark so you can dodge at the last minute if it comes for you; in desperation strike the shark with your elbow locked to stiffen your arm or try kicking it; if you have a knife and the shark is definitely attacking, aim for the eyes or gills (remember an attacking shark covers its eyes with a white nictitating membrane to protect them from attack).

If someone has been attacked by a shark they will probably have a large area of slashed and damaged tissue that will bleed profusely. After the victim is safely out of reach of the shark and at no risk of drowning, try to stem the flow of blood with pressure, tourniquets or firm bandages. To maximise the flow of blood to the brain, position the victim so that his or her head is lower than the feet. Speak calmly and encouragingly, and get help as quickly as you can.

Other animals

Platypus

Australia's famous platypus can, surprisingly, inflict a painful sting. The male has poisonous spurs inside each back leg which he can drive together with some force to penetrate the victim's skin. Swelling and severe pain can result and last for several days, but no deaths have been reported. Leave the wound alone, keep the injured limb still and get medical assistance.

Feral animals

Feral water buffalo, cattle and feral pigs can endanger humans in rare circumstances and should be treated with respect. If you see one, make sure you have somewhere safe to retreat to in case they charge or attack, especially if the animal has young. Feral pigs are scattered throughout Australia, especially in Queensland and New South Wales, and to the north-east of Darwin. They can be infected with a variety of parasites, including spargana, which is a threat to humans. Any meat from a feral pig must be thoroughly cooked to make sure the parasite is killed. Water buffalo, once common in the Top End, are now rare following concerted efforts to exterminate them. They may be infected with tuberculosis.

SUMMARY

- ❑ Know how to read a map and take a suitable one when you travel.
- ❑ Learn how to use a compass and allow for variations from true north.
- ❑ You can navigate roughly by:
  - the sun using a stake or your watch
  - the moon
  - the stars
- ❑ If you are lost, *don't panic, stop*.
- ❑ Revise your route and your map.
- ❑ Make your position obvious.
- ❑ Mark your trail and direction.
- ❑ Be alert to any helpful signs.
- ❑ Always notify someone of your intended journey and your return.

10 DIRECTION FINDING

Knowing where you are, where you want to go, and how to get there can mean the difference between surviving and perishing. You will also need to know how to get your bearing again if you stray off your course, as people who spend a lot of time in the bush inevitably do. To navigate successfully you need to know how to read a map, how to use a compass, and, ideally, how to read the countryside and the heavens.

Map

It is worth revising some fundamentals of map-reading so that you know not only how to read a map, but what sort of map is appropriate for a particular journey.

Scale

The most common scale for bushwalking maps is 1:50 000, which means that 1 unit on the map equals 50 000 units on the ground, for example, 1 cm on the map equals 50 000 cm or 500 m of terrain. Although not everything on the map will be exactly to scale – rivers and roads may be a standard width, say – you will still be able to work out distances more or less accurately.

To measure distance along a relatively straight route, lay the straight edge of a piece of paper along the route on your map and mark the distance between the beginning and end of it. Then lay the marked paper against the scale and read off the distance. If your route twists and turns you can still get a reasonably accurate reading by breaking the route up into a series of straight lines. Lay the straight edge of the paper at the start of the route and mark a point on both the paper and the map at the end of the first straight length, where the route makes its first major turn. Then move the straight edge round till it follows the route again, aligning the two marks, and place another mark where the next major curve or bend occurs. Depending on your needs, you can be meticulous and follow every twist and turn of the track, or you can work out a rough estimate of the distance by cutting or smoothing out the odd corner or wiggle in the route. Once you have followed the route to its end, marking both map and paper as you go, place the paper against the scale and read off the distance.

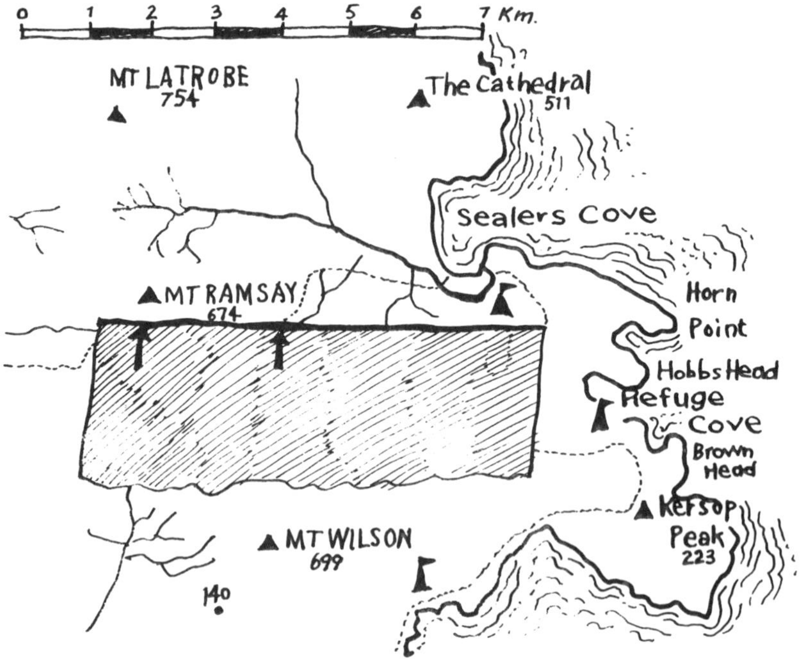

Measuring distance with a straight edge.

If you don't have a straight edge of paper, you can use string, a ruler, a long straight leaf, or dividers.

If you are in hilly country, keep in mind that a gradient of 45° increases the distance by roughly 4 per cent or 4 m over a distance of 100 m.

If you are estimating how far you can travel in a day, remember that a person can walk between fifteen and twenty-five kilometres a day in easy country, but half of that through difficult country.

Contours

Contour lines join points at the same distance above sea level, thereby indicating the way the land rises and falls and the steepness of slopes. If the contour lines are close together, the slope is steep; if they are far apart, the slope is gentle; if they are really crammed together, the country will be extremely steep, although there is usually a separate symbol for cliffs.

The vertical distance between each contour line is called the contour interval. If, for example, this interval is 50 m, then every time you cross a contour line you will have risen 50 m.

Contour lines will also tell you, for example, the shape of a hill. If they are evenly spaced, the hill will rise evenly. If you read from the highest point to the lowest and find that the spacing between the contour lines decreases, the slope will be convex; if it increases, it will be concave.

With practice, you can tell at a glance where the head of a valley and the foot of a spur are located on a map: the V formed by the contours of a valley will point towards the head of the valley, and the V formed by the contours of a spur will point towards the foot of the spur.

Contour lines will give you an idea of the gradient (the slope of the land expressed in figures), but it is best not to rely on the rise or fall of land between just two contour lines. If possible, measure gradient over several contour lines. To do this, measure the distance and write it down with a line above it (let's say it is 500 m). Next, read off the difference in height and write that above the line (say, 50 m). You then divide the first number by the second (500/50) which gives you the gradient (10, or a gradient of 1 in 10). In our example, the slope of 1 in 10 would be too steep for a normal bicycle.

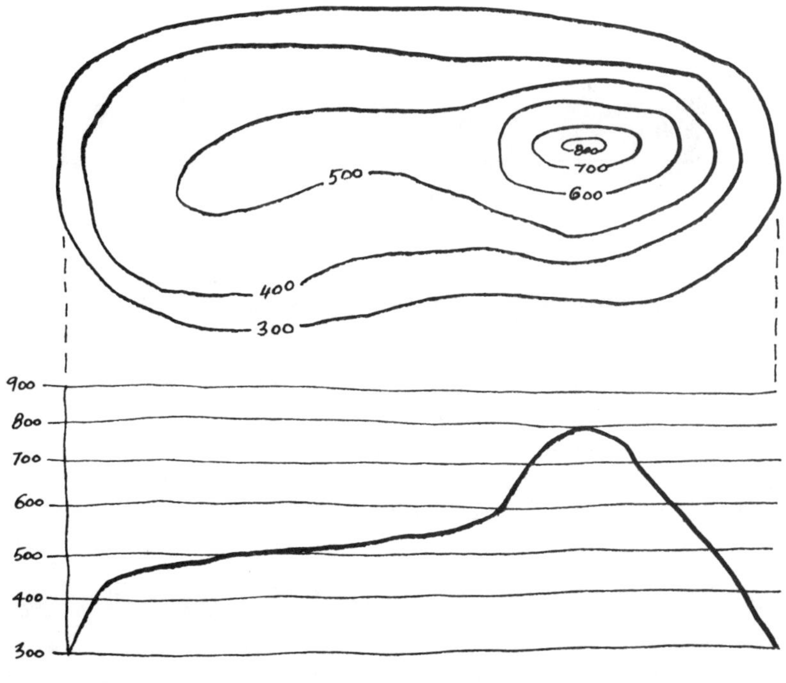

As a rough guide, a person has to climb or clamber up a 1 in 1 slope; they can walk up a 1 in 2 slope; just manage to drive a car up a 1 in 3 slope; ride a bicycle on slopes between 1 in 20 and 1 in 10; and just manage to drive a train up a 1 in 40 slope.

Grid lines

The grid overlaying a map can give you useful information. Grid lines are commonly 1000 m or 1 km apart, and can give you a quick rough guide to the distance you want to travel. The vertical grid lines are also aligned north-south, although there is a slight difference between true north and the north of the grid lines. (This difference is usually expressed in a north-arrow diagram somewhere on the map, along with magnetic north, and is only significant for very careful and detailed compass work.)

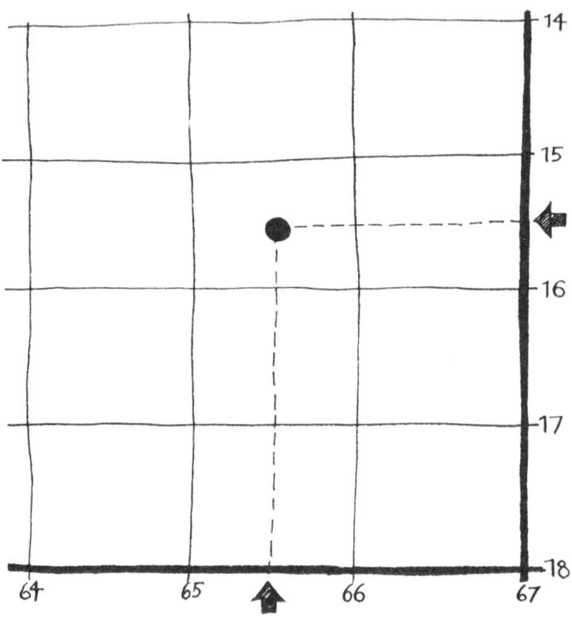

You can identify any point on a map with a grid reference or pair of coordinates. To do this, drop a line straight down to the line reference at the bottom of the map and note down the number to the left. Next, run a horizontal line from the point to the line references at the side of the map and note down the number below your line. Similarly, you can locate any point on a map if you are given the coordinates or grid reference. The example above has been simplified; coordinates usually consist of six numbers, for example 655155, which means references 65.5 and 15.5. The first three numbers refer to the vertical grid line, the last three to the horizontal grid line. The decimal point is left out, but nevertheless the third and sixth numbers always refer to points marked in tenths from any grid line.

Symbols

Various symbols are used on maps, and they should all be included in a key. If you are unsure of a symbol, check it, otherwise you could end up leading your party into a swamp at nightfall when you thought those little tufty symbols meant grassland.

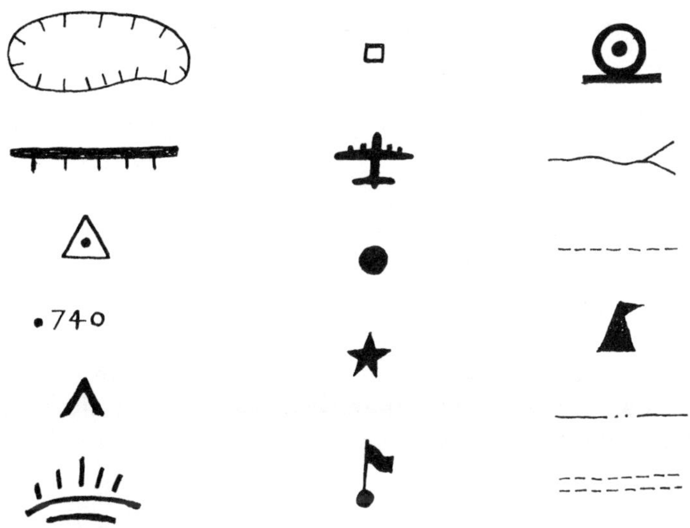

Compass

A compass is simple enough to use, but its use is difficult to describe simply. If someone can explain it to you with compass in hand it would be better than relying entirely on this or any other book.

The cardinal points on the compass – north, south, east and west – can be expressed in degrees round a circle. If north is 0° or 360°, east is 90°, south 180° and west 270°. Bearings are directions quoted in degrees, for example a bearing of 45° is north-east, 225° is south-west.

The compass needle will point to magnetic north unless it is influenced by iron ore in the ground, or a vehicle or steel equipment nearby – even a steel watch band, keys or large buckle could influence a reading, so remove them before you begin.

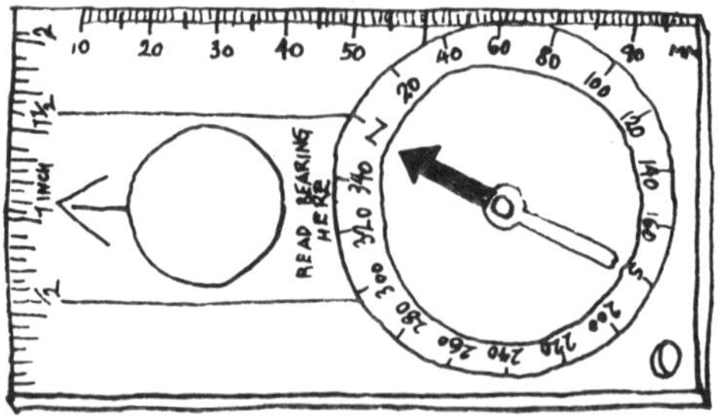

North ain't north

Unfortunately, north is not simply north. There is true north, magnetic north and grid north.

True north

True north is geographical north – the true north pole, that point round which the Earth rotates on its axis.

Magnetic north

A compass needle points to magnetic north, or the magnetic north pole, which is in northern Canada. Magnetic north and true north only coincide for a few places around the globe. Magnetic north also changes slowly but regularly each year.

Grid north

Grid north is the point used by the map maker to construct the grid on the map. Its relationship to true north varies.

Map to terrain and back again

The reason these different norths are important, is that they must be taken into account when you are transferring a compass bearing from a map to the ground or vice versa. If you take a compass bearing on a trig point, say, you will have to convert it to a grid bearing before you plot your course to the trig point on your map. Similarly, a bearing on a map will have to be converted to a magnetic bearing before it can be used with a compass. To do this, you add or subtract the magnetic variation, depending on the information on your map.

You may notice on a map a north-arrow diagram like this:

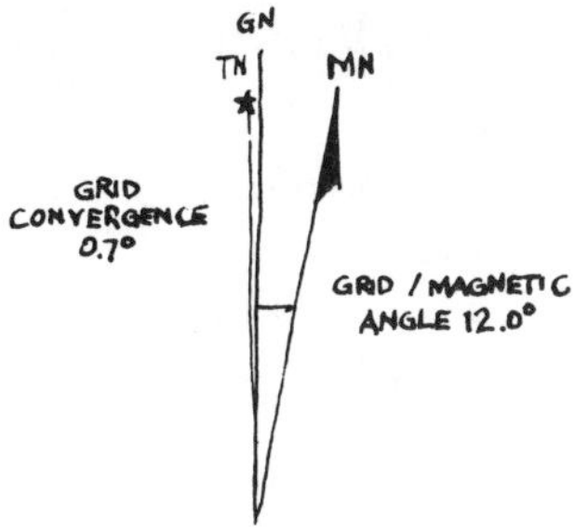

Beneath it may be a note similar to this:

Magnetic north is correct for 1975
and moves easterly by 0.1°
in about three years.

If you are using an old map, you will have to take this rate of change into account should you have to navigate very precisely. For example, the map above was correct for 1975, but if you wanted to use it in the year 1996, 21 years later, you would have to add or subtract 0.7° to the magnetic variation (21/3 years = 7; 7 x 0.1° = 0.7°). Remember for magnetic variations to the east of true north you *add* when starting from a magnetic bearing (i.e. a bearing taken from your compass) and *subtract* when starting from a grid bearing (i.e. a bearing taken from your map). The reverse is the case for variations to the west of true north. Make sure you add or subtract the 0.7° to the magnetic variation printed on your map and not to the compass bearing.

Compass and map orientation

Place your compass over the arrows on the map, aligning the direction of travel arrow with the grid north line so that it is pointing at grid north. Holding both map and compass in position, move the map until the compass needle points north along the line of the orienting arrow.

Bearing from terrain

If you can identify a landmark, face it and position the compass so that the direction of travel arrow points towards it. Move the compass housing (but not the base plate) until the orienting arrow aligns with the red tip of the magnetic needle. Read off the magnetic bearing of your landmark from the dial.

Bearings from terrain are useful if you want to find out where you are on your map and you can identify a couple of landmarks. They are also useful if you want to reach a landmark that will remain visible.

Bearing from your map

Once you have established where you want to go, place the compass on the map so that one edge is aligned with your intended route. Move the compass housing (not the base plate) until the orienting arrow runs parallel with the grid lines and points north. If you have to adjust for magnetic north, place the compass over the north-arrow diagram and align the orienting arrow with the grid north line. Turn the dial (but not the base plate) till the orienting arrow points to magnetic north. Now, keep the dial setting as it is and hold the compass flat, turning it until the red end of the magnetic needle points north over the orienting arrow. The direction of travel arrow will point to where you want to go.

No map? No compass?

In an emergency you may find yourself without either a map or a compass. It is still possible to work out directions from the land around you and the sky above.

Sun

The sun is the most obvious guide – it rises more or less in the east and sets more or less in the west. It crosses the sky from due east to due west only at the two equinoxes in March and September; in December it goes from south-east to south-west, and in June it goes from north-east to north-west. In the southern hemisphere, the sun at noon is usually at due north (don't forget to allow for daylight saving). In the northern hemisphere the sun at noon is usually due south. If for some reason you don't know what hemisphere you are in, shadows move clockwise in the north and anti-clockwise in the south.

Another method for establishing the position of the cardinal points is to drive a stick into a flat piece of cleared ground. Mark the point where the shadow ends about an hour before noon, then several times until about an hour after noon. Join these points to form a curved line. If you run a straight line through these, like the string of a bow, you will have a rough east-west line. At right angles to this will be the north-south line.

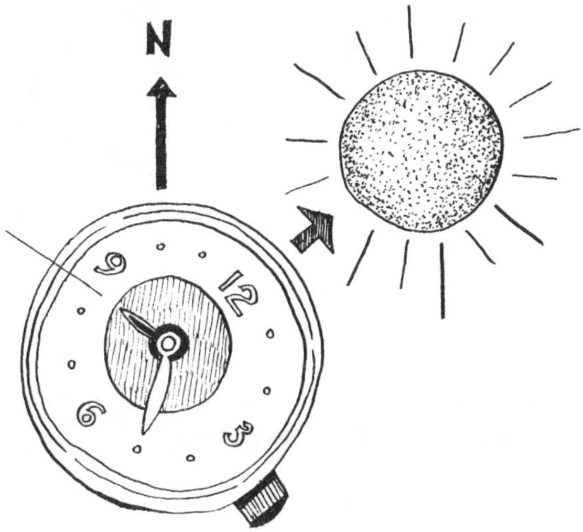

If you are wearing an analogue watch (not a digital) you can use the sun to establish north and south. In the southern hemisphere, point twelve towards the sun, holding the watch level. Halfway between the twelve and the hour hand is the north-south line. In the northern hemisphere, you point the hour hand at the sun then divide the angle between it and twelve to find the north-south line. In overcast conditions, hold a match above the twelve so that the shadow runs down towards the six, then bisect the angle between the shadow and the hour hand to find the north-south line.

Night sky

In the southern hemisphere, the Southern Cross can help you find south. Make sure you are looking at the real Southern Cross and not one of the other cross-shaped constellations by locating the two pointer stars. Another way to locate the Southern Cross is to look for the Coal Sack, a dark patch in the Milky Way directly above the south pole; the Southern Cross is to one side of it.

Having located the Southern Cross and the pointers, run an imaginary line down the long axis of the Cross and another one at right angles to a line joining the pointers. Where these two lines intersect is celestial south, and if you drop a line to the horizon from this point you will locate south.

The moon can give you a rough guide to east and west: if it rises before the sun has set, the light side will be roughly west; if it rises after midnight, the light side will be roughly east.

Lost

If you are lost, there are several important things to remember, but before we tackle them, it is worth noting a few of the ways you can avoid getting lost in the first place.

If you are intending to walk to your destination and return by the same route, you can increase your chances of returning home safely by turning round at regular intervals on the way out and taking note of what you see. This will be your view when you are returning, and if you have noted landmarks in the foreground and the distance, you will be able to check if you are travelling in the right direction. This advice sounds obvious, but it is surprising how few people think to do it, and how different is the view on the outward journey from the view on the return journey.

On any journey it is useful to keep notes or a sketch map: record the distances you have travelled and the direction as well as the landmarks you have passed. If you are travelling through country with few landmarks, you can make a few of your own by laying heavy branches side by side or lines of stones in the direction of travel, by overturning large rocks or building a small cairn on high ground, and even by breaking or bending a branch.

If you find that you no longer know where you are, *stop* and think. *Do not panic.* If you have been following a map, check it carefully to make sure the ground you have just covered is the ground you identified on the map. Such a simple expedient may help you see that you have gone down a different ridge or spur or identified the wrong rocky outcrop or something similar. If this revision does not help, carefully retrace your steps until you come to a landmark you can definitely identify. Do not press on in the hope that the landmark you were heading for is just over the next rise; do not press on if night is falling or the weather has turned nasty, or anyone in your party is unfit to travel – it is safer to camp for an extra night, eat some food and tackle the problem in the morning.

When you know you are lost, *don't panic – stop*. If you have not revised your route and checked your map, then do so now. A view from a high point (a hill or even a tree) may make things clearer. But if none of this helps, stay put and make some sort of camp while there is still light. Try to make your camp as obvious as possible so you can be located easily by rescuers. Spread out anything bright or shiny or colourful; light a bright fire at night time and a smoking one during the day.

If you are forced to go for help, leave signs of your camp, of the direction you have taken and mark your trail as you go. If you can leave a note, so much the better. If water is a problem, throw away anything rather than water to lighten your load, even food. In hot weather, travel at night or in the cooler times of the day. Walk carefully and conserve your strength, don't blunder about and exhaust or injure yourself. Watch out for tracks and follow them, again marking your route. Use all your senses to read the country through which you are travelling – can you hear or smell water? smoke? habitation? Are birds, insects or animals showing you the way to water? Remember to keep looking back to memorise landmarks and note landmarks ahead of you.

Obviously no-one will know you are lost unless you informed someone of your intended route and time of return. This should be done before any journey. When you return, you must notify that person so that they are not organising a search party in vain or continuing to search once you are safe.

SUMMARY

- ❑ Overhaul your vehicle before a journey.
- ❑ Carry:
  - extra water
  - extra fuel and oil
  - adequate spare parts
  - toolkit
  - camping gear
- ❑ A bull bag will jack up a vehicle in sand.
- ❑ Bury an anchor for a winch if there are no trees or rocks.
- ❑ Don't leave a stranded vehicle unless you absolutely must.
- ❑ A vehicle provides many survival and signalling necessities.
- ❑ A small space is easiest to heat.
- ❑ In a sinking car, doors can be opened when water pressure on either side of the door is equal.

11 VEHICLES

So long as your vehicle is in good working order, you can be almost anywhere in Australia and still be reasonably safe. But as soon as it breaks down or becomes stuck, you need only be on an isolated stretch of road to find yourself in trouble. When your survival depends on a vehicle, it is easier to prevent problems than to cure them, so make sure you and your vehicle are well prepared.

Outback driving

Before you go on a long journey away from settled areas, have your car thoroughly overhauled so that it is in good mechanical order. Make sure the tyres have plenty of tread on them and check the condition of the spare(s).

Your vehicle should carry a good selection of the following, plus any special requirements for the country through which you will be travelling:

- ❑ drinking water (at least 10-15 litres per person per day and then some)
- ❑ extra fuel (possibly up to double what you would need because of the extra used when driving through sand, mud or floods) and oil in approved containers
- ❑ a bull bag or jack with steel or redgum base plate
- ❑ spare wheel(s)
- ❑ tyre tubes (2)
- ❑ winch
- ❑ tyre chains (if travelling through snow), antifreeze
- ❑ dewatering agent
- ❑ wheel chock
- ❑ good tool kit and selected spare parts:
    - fan belt
    - fuel filter
    - radiator hoses
    - distributor points
    - spark plugs
    - coil
    - condenser
    - tyre change tools (tyre levers, etc.)

  - tyre repair kit
  - tyre pump
  - tyre gauge
  - tow cable
  - pliers
  - hacksaw
  - screwdrivers
  - tape for engine hoses
  - valves, nuts, bolts, etc.
  - file
  - wrench set
- ❑ collapsible spade
- ❑ machete, tomahawk or axe
- ❑ bushman's saw
- ❑ water bucket
- ❑ plastic sheet
- ❑ space blanket(s)
- ❑ tarpaulin
- ❑ torch
- ❑ one week's food
- ❑ camping gear

Bogged

If you are bogged in sand or mud, *stop*, get out and assess the situation. You will see whether it is better to try to drive out forwards or to reverse out, and you will have avoided spinning the wheels so much that the vehicle sinks even further. If you think you can drive out, have someone push the car while you drive out using as little acceleration as possible and pulling the handbrake half on to avoid spinning the wheels.

If this does not work, let the tyres down by half to increase traction. If you are still bogged, dig away the mud or sand from in front of the driving wheels to form a smooth slope. Cover the slope with sacks, wood, car mats or anything else that will increase traction. Point the steering wheels straight forward, and try to drive out once more, using the accelerator as little as possible. If you do manage to drive out, reinflate your tyres with your own pump or travel very slowly until you reach a service station with air.

If you have nothing to place under your jack, remove a hubcap and use that. A bull bag can also help free a bogged car. This strong tough bag can be inflated by attaching it to the exhaust and idling the engine for a minute or so. Place the bag under the vehicle with a rug or mat over it to protect it from sharp edges or a hot exhaust. If, for example, you want to push the car out forwards, place the bag at the back. If the car has to move sideways, place a chock against the wheel on which the car will pivot. When the bag is inflated, push the car onto solid ground or place material under the tyres that will increase traction then try to drive out.

The bull bag can also be used as a jack in sand or where the surface is too soft to support a jack.

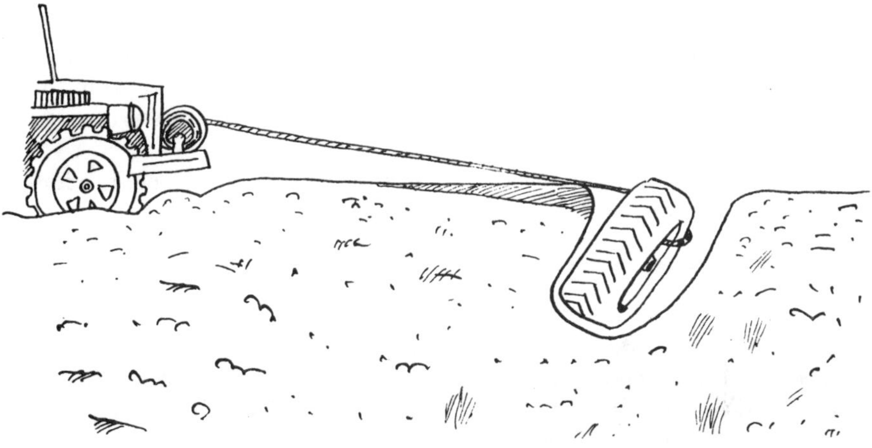

If you have a winch on your vehicle but there is no tree or rock nearby to attach it to, consider digging a trench and placing an anchor of some kind in it, such as a log, tyre or large rock. The anchor should be below ground level, and a slit trench should be dug from the anchor to the vehicle to take the cable or rope. Make sure the anchor cannot fly out of the trench by undercutting the trench on the side nearest the vehicle.

Tyres

If you have to repair a tyre, especially one from a heavy vehicle such as a four-wheel drive, you can break the seal by aligning the side of the tyre with the wheel and driving the vehicle back and forth over it. It is also possible to buy commercial tyre seal breakers. If you have a tyre repair kit and spare tubes, even a bad puncture should be fixable.

Overheating

If possible, stop and allow the engine to cool. Don't remove the radiator cap until the engine is cool or you could be scalded. If you can't stop, turn on the heater; it will make you very uncomfortable, but it will cool the engine slightly.

Check that the radiator was topped up with water, and if not, add some, but make sure the engine is running before you do so. If you know you put water in the radiator, check carefully for a leak in both the radiator and hoses. Egg white or wheat cereals mixed into the radiator water will seal small holes, and there are commercial products that will do the same.

If there is a leak in a water hose, plug the hole any way you can then wrap it in cloth and finally in electrical tape. Remove the cap from the radiator to reduce pressure and proceed slowly, keeping the engine revs low.

Overheating may cause vapour locks in the fuel lines. Cool the fuel lines, carburettor and fuel pump with wet rags and fanning.

Trapped in water

If you are trapped in a vehicle in deep water, *don't panic*. Cars do not usually sink immediately, so you should have time to free yourself from seatbelts and attend to any children or incapacitated people in the vehicle. If the car has not stabilised, leave your seatbelts on and wait till it does. If it is drifting rather than sinking, wait till it reaches shallow water or comes close to the bank before you escape.

If you can escape through a window before the car starts to sink, then do so at once. If you can't, close all the windows and air vents to keep the water out for as long as possible. If the doors are tightly closed because of water pressure or an accident, wait until the car slowly fills with water. This will equalise the water pressure on both sides of the door and make it possible to open a door to escape. You can usually do this before the water reaches your chin. Make sure everyone is able to keep their heads above water and help those who can't. Turn on the headlamps to make the car easier to locate.

The heavier end of the car, usually the front, will probably sink first, so climb into the back seat to make the most of the trapped air for as long as possible. People have survived on this air for up to twenty minutes, so there is no need to panic and rush into leaving the car before you can do so safely.

Unlock the door or doors through which you will escape, and keep your hand on the door handle until everyone is ready and you are able to open the door. Try to keep hold of each other's clothes or limbs as you leave the car so that no one is lost. Take a deep breath, hold your nose and keep your mouth closed, and help children to do the same as you swim for the surface. Check that everyone has reached the surface and then that they are able to reach the shore.

If the doors and windows are impossible to open for some reason, kick out the windscreen or back window.

Surviving with a vehicle

If your vehicle breaks down, stay with it unless you have a *very* good reason for leaving, such as no drinking water because of additives in the radiator water. If you do decide to leave your vehicle, make large clear signs near it, ideally big enough to be seen from an aircraft, indicating the direction you have taken. Leave a note somewhere safe and obvious in the vehicle explaining when and why you left, which way you were headed, how many of you are in the party and the condition of each member.

If you have no good reason to leave your vehicles, stay put. It is much easier to find than you will be. A car, van, truck or downed aircraft can provide you with many of the necessities for survival, such as shelter from extremes of temperature, and water, so long as the radiator water contains no additives such as antifreeze, hole-filling solution or anti-rust solution. Rescuers can be signalled with a mirror or bright metal, with headlights, or by burning a tyre or oily rags. (See the section on signals for more ways of using a vehicle to signal rescuers.)

Snowbound vehicle

Stay with your vehicle unless you absolutely have to try to reach help. Even properly dressed for snow travel, you may be unable to reach a settlement before you are exhausted, that is if you don't become lost. However cold it may be outside, leave the window open a crack so you don't suffocate. In extreme conditions, below -10°C, the metal of a vehicle will conduct heat out into the environment so quickly that you will be better off sheltering nearby, even in the snow. Make sure you leave a note giving careful and accurate directions to your shelter, even if it is only a metre or two away from the vehicle. If you are forced to seek shelter nearby, use any remaining fuel to run the heater so that you can return periodically and thaw out while you are making your shelter. Check that the exhaust pipe is not blocked and that the vehicle is adequately ventilated.

Remember that the smaller the shelter the easier it is to keep warm. This applies to vehicles as well. If you are in really dire circumstances, rip down the vehicle's lining and insulation and strip the seat covers to use as a small 'tent' either inside your vehicle or in your nearby snow shelter if you are forced to evacuate.

Not only do vehicles supply a number of signalling devices, they can also supply you with fuel and flame for a fire. Signal your whereabouts by burning a spare tyre or an oil-soaked rag. A hubcap or other metal container can be used as a small fireplace in which to burn sand or soil soaked in petrol. If you do not have matches, remove the battery and cross wires from each pole to make a spark.

Remember that very cold metal can freeze your skin and tear it off. If you cannot wear gloves to perform a particular task, cover your fingers with adhesive tape.

Radios

Many people travelling in the outback have a CB radio with which to request assistance or communicate with other drivers. A UHF radio is another possibility, although it sends a 'straight-line' signal. The most powerful and expensive radio is the VHF, which is used by the Flying Doctor Service and can be rented from them more cheaply than the cost of buying one outright.

Assorted emergencies

Fuel

If you are running low on petrol, slow down to round 50 kilometres per hour and coast down hills. Rather than use too much accelerator, change down a gear.

If you flood the engine when trying to start it, hold the accelerator down but do not pump it.

If the petrol tank springs a leak, you can plug the hole with soap.

Brakes

If the brake line on hydraulic brakes is broken, crimp it between the leak and the hydraulic pump. Use low gear and the handbrake to help you stop and only proceed with extreme caution.

Battery

If the battery is flat, you can start a manual vehicle by pushing it down a slope or towing it. Depress the clutch, put the vehicle into second gear and release the clutch when it has picked up enough speed to turn the engine over.

Traction

If you lose traction when driving through sand, mud or snow, you may be able to improve a vehicle's performance by redistributing weight so that it is over the drive wheels.

SUMMARY

- ❑ Universal distress signals include:
  - Mayday
  - SOS (• • • - - - • • •)
  - A group of any three signals repeated after one minute
- ❑ Make use of vehicle parts and fuel to signal.
- ❑ Collect material for signal fires and keep dry.
- ❑ Site signals where they can be clearly seen.
- ❑ Learn Morse code, semaphore or other signalling system.

12 SIGNALS

There are a number of signalling systems that are understood internationally, but the first and most important signal you will ever send is the one that tells someone of your existence. To do this you can use anything at your disposal, so long as you catch the attention of someone and, if necessary, make it known that you need help.

Two well-known distress signals are:

- SOS – Save Our Souls, and
- Mayday – from *M'aidez*, French for help me.

A group of any three signals also indicates distress, whether it be three mirror flashes, fires, whistles, cairns, cooees, etc. Leave one minute between each group of three signals.

If you are trying to signal an aircraft and it appears not to have seen you, watch the direction it takes. It may be making regular sweeps of an area, into and away from the sun. Once you understand its pattern you will know when to signal it again.

Signalling materials

Aircraft, cars and other vehicles provide a variety of signalling options. The rear-vision mirror or side mirrors, or even a shiny piece of chrome, metal or glass can be used for signalling during the day. A deflated tyre can be burnt to provide plenty of thick black smoke. Similarly a rag or foliage soaked in sump oil, hydraulic fluid, fuel or oil can be burned. Any bright materials such as life jackets, parachutes, tarpaulins or seat covers can be spread out on the ground to attract attention.

At night time, so long as the power in the battery has been conserved, the headlights can be taken out and reconnected to the battery to shine into the sky or towards rescuers. Wait till you are sure someone is there before using up precious power. You can also sound or signal with the horn.

You can also make use of natural materials. Many green leaves or plants will give off thick smoke when they are burned. But some species, those full of volatile oils such as certain Australian acacias, will burst into flame and produce very little smoke even when they are freshly cut. Unless you are going to run yourself short of fire-lighting material, experiment with surrounding plants to see how they burn and the colour of their smoke. Once you have established which is the best foliage for a signal, collect large piles of it to build signal fires. This should be done as soon as you have tended to injuries and set up a suitable shelter. You should have extra fuel at hand (green foliage, rubber, oil, etc.) in case your first signal fire is not successful.

If there is a small tree a good distance from other vegetation, it can serve as a signal. Set dry material amongst the branches so that they will catch fire and burn. Make sure there is no danger of starting a bushfire. A dead tree can serve a similar purpose, but it may burn for a long time, and in dry, hot or windy weather become a fire hazard.

Take note of the colour of the surrounding countryside. If you are in snow, light-coloured sand or similar pale surroundings, burn oil or rubber to produce dark smoke. If you are amongst dark plants and trees, green vegetation or wet fabric will produce pale smoke.

Siting signals

If you are sending visual signals, the site you choose is important, especially if you are signalling to an aircraft. Choose high ground, such as the top of a hill or ridge, so that your signal will not be sheltered from any direction by neighbouring high ground. If you are in timbered country, choose a site such as a clearing where the tree canopy will not obscure your signal.

If you are signalling with fire, and fuel is not a problem, set three signal fires in an equilateral triangle. They should be ready to burn at any moment, should you hear a search plane or search party. Keep them dry and well maintained.

To start a fire quickly, use tinder, petrol or other suitable fuel, but *do not* pour or throw it on the fire. *Never* do this. Soak a rag or something similar in petrol and put it amongst the tinder. Remove the fuel container to a safe distance *at once*, before you light the fire. Pause for a moment or two and then light the fire. If it doesn't light, rake the fire apart to check for sparks before you add more petrol-soaked fuel.

Codes

The following codes can be used to set up permanent signals on the ground for aircraft; they need no maintenance and can be seen whether you are awake or asleep, injured or fit. Some of them are useful for search parties to communicate with other groups or with aircraft.

Make the symbols large and clear. Ideally, they should be 10 m long and 3 m wide, with a 3 m break between symbols. Use anything to hand

– boughs, wreckage, stones – or dig or trample a trench. Make light work for you by building up the sides of your symbols to cast a shadow.

I	serious injury; need doctor or casualty evacuation
II	need medical supplies
F	need food and water
X	unable to move
L	need fuel and oil
N	no; negative
Y	yes
A	yes; affirmative
K	indicate direction to proceed
→	moving in this direction
JL	do not understand
LL	all is well
□	need compass and map
△	probably safe to land
	attempting take-off
!	need radio/signal lamp/battery
	aircraft badly damaged

LLL	operation completed
	found all personnel
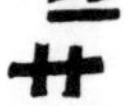	found some personnel
XX	unable to continue; returning to base
	divided into two groups, each proceeding in direction indicated
→→	information received that aircraft in this direction
NN	nothing found; will continue search

Aircraft responses

If your message has been seen and understood, an aircraft will rock from side to side if visibility is good or, at night or if visibility is poor, signal with green flashes. If your message has been seen but not understood, an aircraft will make a complete right-hand or clockwise circle in good visibility; in poor visibility it will signal with red flashes.

Morse code

You can transmit a message in Morse code by waving a flag or using a flashing light or mirror flashes. To be sure you are directing mirror flashes accurately, put your hand in line between the mirror and what you are trying to contact, while holding the mirror close to your eyes. Flash onto your hand, and then move your hand away and send the signal.

If you are using a flag, you will move it to the left for dashes and to the right for dots. Make sure movements to the left (dashes) are slightly longer than movements to the right (dots). At a distance, make a figure of eight to left and right as appropriate; up close this may be unnecessary.

Letters

A • -
B - • • •
C - • - •
D - • •
E •
F • • - •
G - - •
H • • • •
I • •
J • - - -
K - • -
L • - • •
M - -
N - •
O - - -
P • - - •
Q - - • -
R • - •
S • • •
T -
U • • -
V • • • -
W • - -
X - • • -
Y - • - -
Z - - • •

Figures

1 • - - - -
2 • • - - -
3 • • • - -
4 • • • • -
5 • • • • •
6 - • • • •
7 - - • • •
8 - - - • •
9 - - - - •
0 - - - - -

Words

SOS • • • - - - • • •
Help • • • • | • | • - • • | • - - •
Lost • - • • | - - - | • • • | -
Injury • • | - • | • - - - | • • - | • - • | - • - -
Doctor - • • | - - - | - • - • | - | - - - | • - •
Water • - - | • - | - | • | • - •
Food • • - • | - - - | - - - | - • •

If you are sending or receiving messages there are several codes for useful phrases. Some of them should be sent as a single word without pauses (these are set in italics below), others are sent with pauses.

Phrases

Sending signals	
AAAAA, etc.	Call sign. I have a message.
Pause	End of word. More follows.
AAA	End of sentence. More follows.
AR	End of message.
EEEEEEEE, etc.	Error. Start from last correct word.

Receiving signals	
K	I am ready. Start message.
TTTTTT, etc.	I am receiving you.
T	Word received.
IMI	Repeat sign. I do not understand.
R	Message received.

Semaphore

If you have nothing to signal with other than a couple of rags, plastic bags, or even leafy branches, you can still send a message using semaphore. Keep in mind the backdrop to your signalling. If you have light coloured 'flags', you would be better to stand against dark foliage than a pale sky. At night you can still use semaphore if you wrap rags around sticks, soak them in fuel and set fire to them. Make your signals slowly and clearly. If necessary, repeat any words. It is a good idea to learn SOS in semaphore off by heart, even if you cannot memorise all the rest.

A/1
B/2
C/3
D/4
E/5
F/6
G/7
H/8
I/9
J
K/0
L
M
N
O
P
Q
R
S
T
U
V
W
X
Y
Z

Body signals

These signals can convey information to aircraft. Make the signals clearly with big exaggerated movements. Note the changes in position of the body and legs as well as the arms. If you have some sort of flags, hold them to emphasise yes and no gestures.

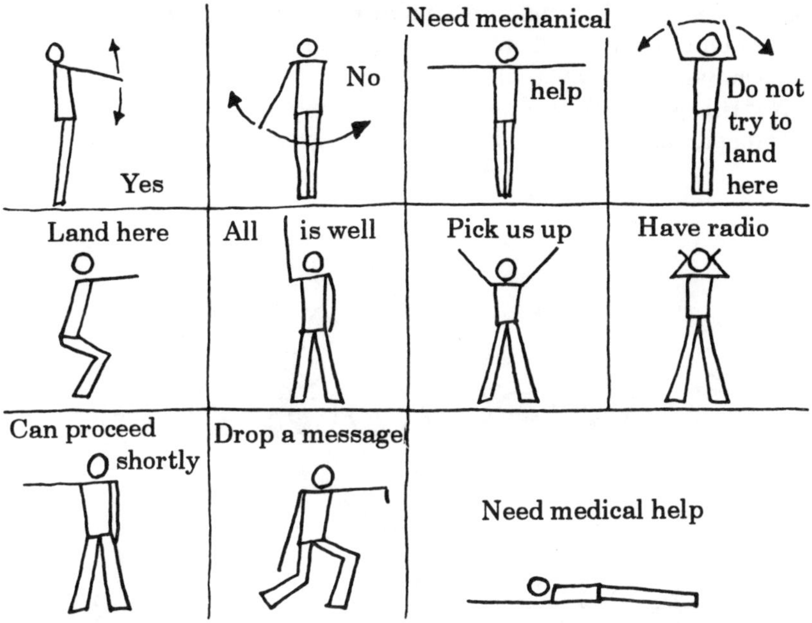

Direction signs

If you have left camp to try to walk out, leave clear signs of the direction you have taken. To do this, make use of sticks, branches, stones and even clumps of grass.

This direction. [arrow, visible from air; branch held in forked stick, top indicating direction; knot in grass clump, top flopping in direction taken; forked stick, single part pointing direction; large stone with smaller on top and small stone beside, latter indicating direction]

Turn. [arrow cut in tree]

Not this way. [sticks crossed]

Danger, emergency. [3 stakes, rocks or grass clumps]

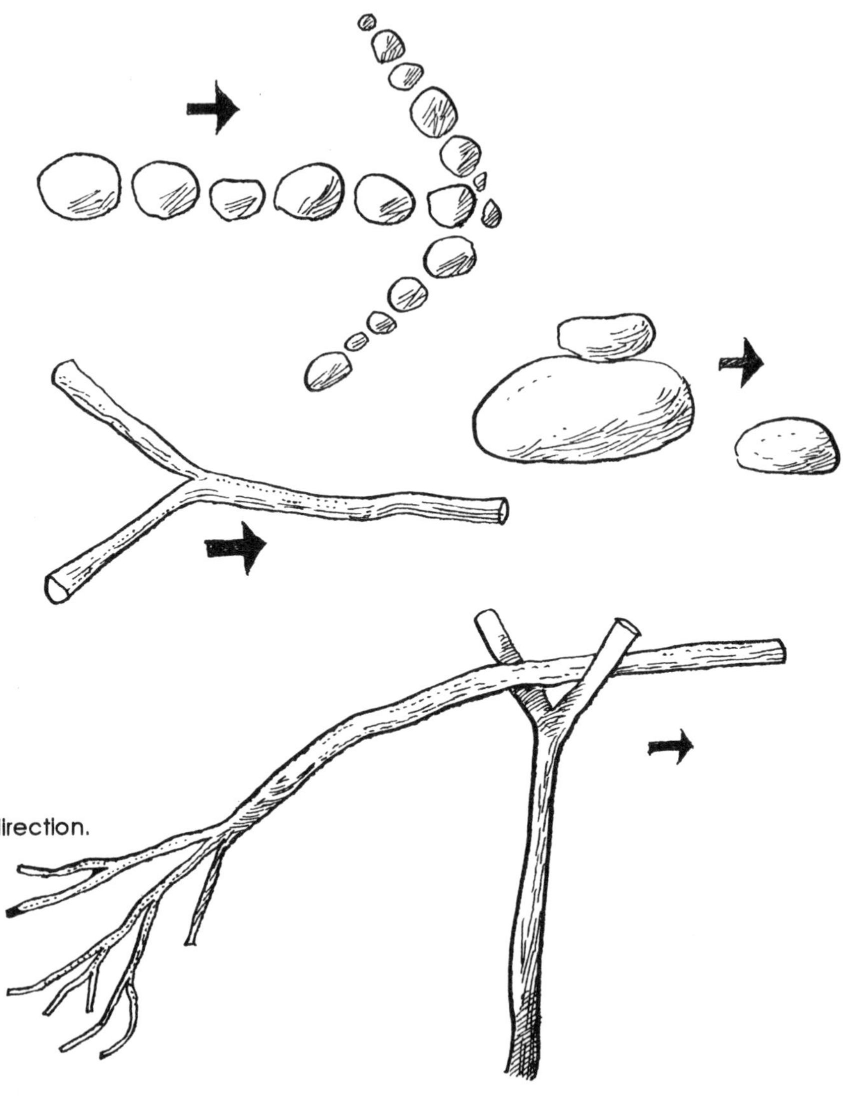

This direction.

Signals at sea

If you find yourself in trouble at sea, you can signal to the shore or to nearby craft using any of the following signals.

Mayday	Repeat this word on the radio.
SOS	Repeat in any manner, over radio, by Morse code (• • • - - - • • •), semaphore, flashing lights, etc.
Foghorn	Sound continuously.
Gun	Fire at 1-minute intervals.
Rockets	Fire those emitting red stars at short intervals.
Flags	Square flag with a ball above or below.
Arms	Raise and lower outstretched arms slowly and repeatedly.
Smoke	Orange smoke.
Flare	Red light.
Fire	Burn something in a barrel to show flames.

INDEX

abdominal wounds 33
aircraft
  responses 127-8
  search 125
  signals 126
alcohol 46, 84
ammunition 22
amphibians 56
animals 5-6
ants 59, 65, 87, 92
  larvae 58-9
arm injuries 35-6
avalanches 68, 77

babies and cold 82, 83, 85
baobab tree 6
battery 22, 122, 123
bearings, compass 110-12
bees 59, 87, 92
birds 5, 55-6, 65
black house spiders 93
bleeding 31-5
  internal 34
blizzards 68, 76
bloodwood 6
blubbers 100
blue bottle 100
blue-ringed octopus 100
body signals 131
bogged 118
bogong moths 59
bones, broken 35-9
bottle tree 6
box jellyfish 87, 100
brakes 123
breathing 26
broken bones 35-9
bull bag 117, 118-19
bulrushes 53
burns 42
bush still 8-9
bushfire 17, 126, *see also* fire
  first aid 40-2
butchering 52-3

cacti 7
camp sites 12-13
candle 20
cane toads 56
cardiac compression, external 29-30
casuarina 6
cattle, feral 103
celestial south 113-14
centipedes 92
chest wounds 33
children
  hypothermia 83, 85
  resuscitation 26-7
chilling 82-5
cicadas 59
cliffs 12
clouds 63-4
coconuts 7
codes 126-33
cold 45-7
  effects 81
coma position 30-1
compass 109-12
  bearings 110-12
condensation 7-9
consciousness 25
contours 106-8
coordinates 108-9
cramps 41, 45
  heat 80, 81
crocodiles 100-1
cyclones 68, 73-4

dangerous creatures 87-95
deadfalls 49, 55
dehydration 40-1
dew 3-4
direction
  finding 105-15
  signs 132
dislocations 39-40
distillation 7-9
dust storms 68, 75

earthquakes 68, 74-5
eating 80, 82
edibility test 56-7
elderly and hypothermia 83, 85
emergency kit vi
ergot 56
eucalypts 6

field mushrooms 58
fire 17-23, 68, 69-71, 122, *see also* bushfire
  lighting, friction 22-3
  signal 125-6, 133
first aid 25-47
fish 5, 53-4
flags 133
flints 21
floods 68, 71-3
fog 63
food 49-59
fractures 35-9
freezing 82-5
friction firelighting 22-3
frogs 6, 56
frostbite 45-6, 83-4
fuel 19-20, 117, 122
fungi 56, 57-8

game 52
gradients 107-8
grasshoppers 59
grid
  lines 108-9
  north 110, 111
  reference 108-9

hair erector muscles 80, 82
head wounds 33
heart beat 29-30
heat 45
  cramps 41, 45, 80, 81
  effects 79-81
  exhaustion 41, 45, 81
  radiant, fires 68, 69 71, 79
heatstroke 41-2, 45, 79, 81
honey 59
hypothermia 46-7, 79, 84-5
  special risk 83, 85

ice 7
infection 34
insects 5, 12, 58-9
internal bleeding 34

jack 117, 118, 119
jellyfish 87
  box 87
  stings 44
Jenner, Edward 65, 67

key 109
killing 52
kindling 19

lamps, slush 53
landslides 12
lateral recovery position, *see* coma position
leg injuries 36
lenses 21
lighters 20-1
lightning 12, 63, 75-6
lizards 55
lost 114-15

maggots 58
magnetic
  bearing 112
  north 108, 110
  variation 111
mammals 51-3
maps 105-9
  symbols 109
march flies 59
matches 20-1
Mayday 124, 125, 133
meat 49-56
medical kit vi-vii
melaleucas 6
mirror signals 128
mist 63
Morse code 128-9, 133
mouth-to-mouth resuscitation 26-7
muscle cramps 41, 45, 80, 81

natural disasters 69-77
nets 51, 53, 55
night sky 113
north 108, 110 *see also* grid north and magnetic north
  arrow diagram 108

orientation 111
outback driving 117-18
overheating 120

palms 7
paper barks 6
pelvis, fractured 37
pigface 53
pigs, feral 103
PIM (Pressure/Immobilisation Method) 42-4, 98, 100
  exceptions 87-9
  summary 86
plants 6
platypus 102
poisoning 57
poisonous
  fish 96
  plants 57
Portuguese man-of war 100
pressure points 32
Pressure/Immobilisation Method *see* PIM
prickly heat 45, 81
puffballs 58
purification 3
purslane 53

radiator water 121
radio 122, 133
rain 3-4, 13, 63
redback spiders 87, 94
reptiles 55
resuscitation 26-7
  rates 24
rivers, flooded 71-3
rock falls 12
rockets 133
rodents 65

salt 40, 41, 45, 80
  water crocodiles 100-1
sand storms 75
scale 105-6
scorpions 93
sea
  creature stings 44-5
  signals 133
  snakes 96
  wasp 100
semaphore 129-30, 133
sharks 101-2
she-oak 6
shelter 11-15
shivering 81
shock 39
signals 125-33

at sea 133
body 131
devices 121-2
direction 132
fires 23, 125-6
sites 126
skull, fractured 37
smoke 125-6, 133
snakes 55, 89-91
bite 42-3, 91
sea 96
snares 49-50, 51, 55
snow 7, 14, 63, 126
blindness 46, 84
storms 76
snowbound vehicles 121-2
solar still 8-9
SOS 124, 125, 128, 129, 133
Southern Cross 113
spiders 93-5
black house 93
redback 87, 94
wolf 94-5
spinal injury 37-9
splints 35-9
sprains 39-40
stills 8-9
stingers 100
stinging fish 89
stingrays 99
stings 44-5
stonefish 89, 99
stings 45
storms 65, 75-6
dust 68
sand 75
snow 76
thunder 65, 68, 75-6
wind 73-4
strains 39-40
stringy barks 6
sun 112-13
sunburn 80-1
sweat 1, 9
sweating 40, 41, 79-80, 81, 82
swifts 65
symbols, map 109

tea-tree 6
temperature extremes 79-85
tents 11, 122
thunder storms 65, 68, 75-6
tickling trout 53
ticks 89, 96
tidal waves 74
tinder 19, 22
toads 56
tourniquet 33, 44, 91, 102
traction 123
traps 49-50, 51, 55
fish 54
trees 6, 12
trench foot 45, 83
trout 53
true north 110
turtles 55
tyres 119-20

unconsciousness 25
urine 33

vehicle 13, 117-23
in cyclones 73
in dust or sand storms 75
in earthquakes 74
in fires 70
signals 125
vines 6-7

walking rates 106
wasps 89, 96
watch 113
water 1-9, 12, 80, 115, 117
buffalo 103
drinking 73, 74, 75
trapped in 120-1
watercress 53
weather 61-7
maps 61-2
signs 63-7
white-outs 76
wind 12, 63
storms 73-4
witchetty grubs 58
wolf spiders 94-5
wounds 33-5